URBAN TRAILS

PENINSULA & SOUTH BAY

URBAN TRAILS
PENINSULA & SOUTH BAY

Pacifica · Silicon Valley · San Jose

ALEXANDRA KENIN

MOUNTAINEERS BOOKS

To my 18th Street family—Brett, Dylan, Maxine, and Jodie

MOUNTAINEERS BOOKS is dedicated to the exploration, preservation, and enjoyment of outdoor and wilderness areas.

1001 SW Klickitat Way, Suite 201, Seattle, WA 98134
800-553-4453, www.mountaineersbooks.org

Printed in China
First edition, 2026

Design: Jen Grable
Layout: Ellis Failor-Rich
Cartographer: Ben Pease, Pease Press
All photographs by the author unless credited otherwise
Cover photograph: Wildflowers and ocean views at Mori Point (Hike 2)
Frontispiece: Sandy Wood Lake in Ed R. Levin County Park (Hike 43)

Library of Congress Cataloging-in-Publication data is available for this title at https://lccn.loc.gov/2025026211; the LC ebook record is available at https://lccn.loc.gov/2025026212.

Mountaineers Books titles may be purchased for corporate, educational, or other promotional sales, and our authors are available for a wide range of events. For information on special discounts or booking an author, contact our customer service at 800-553-4453 or mbooks@mountaineersbooks.org.

Printed on FSC-certified® materials.

MIX
Paper | Supporting responsible forestry
FSC® C188448

ISBN (paperback): 978-1-68051-730-9
ISBN (ebook): 978-1-68051-731-6

An independent nonprofit publisher since 1960

CONTENTS

SOUTHERN PENINSULA

SARATOGA AND LOS GATOS

SAN JOSE AND MILPITAS

MORGAN HILL, COYOTE VALLEY, AND GILROY

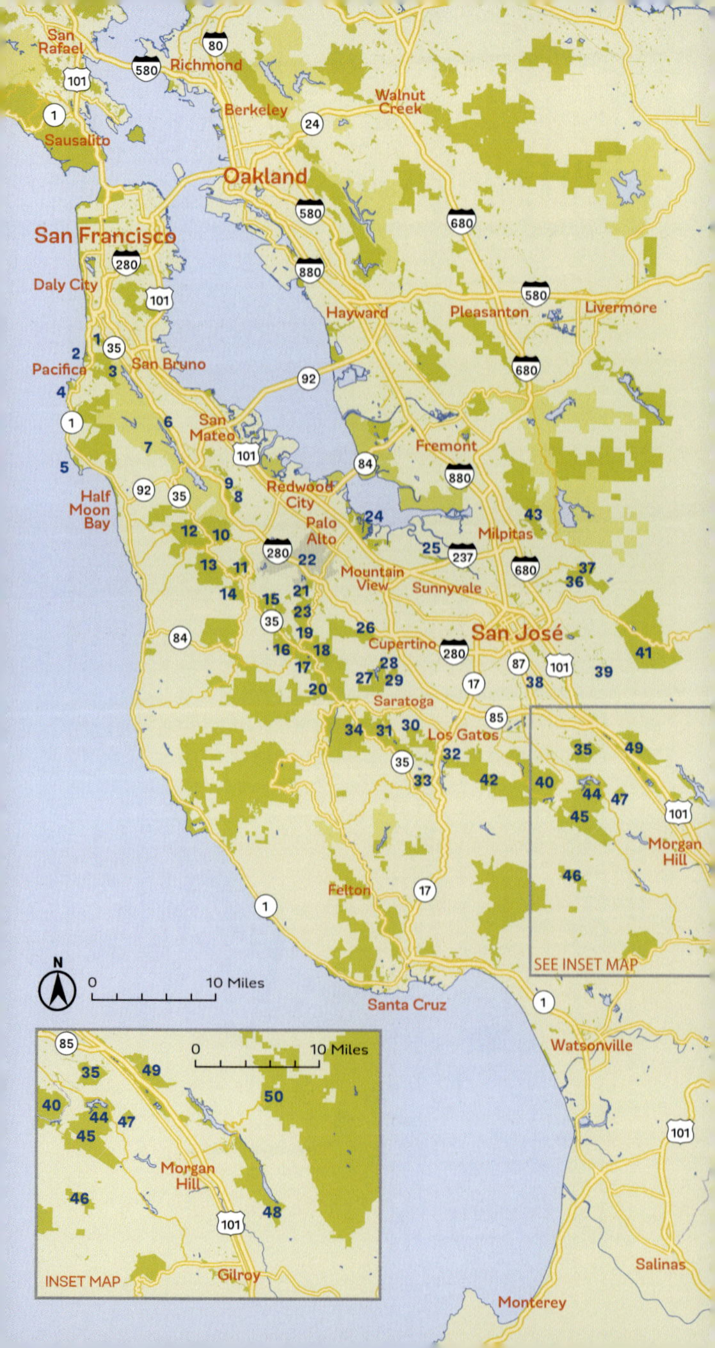

San Rafael
Richmond
Berkeley
Walnut Creek
Sausalito
Oakland
San Francisco
Daly City
Hayward
Pleasanton
Livermore
Pacifica
San Bruno
San Mateo
Fremont
Half Moon Bay
Redwood City
Palo Alto
Milpitas
Mountain View
Sunnyvale
San José
Cupertino
Saratoga
Los Gatos
Morgan Hill
Felton
SEE INSET MAP
10 Miles
Santa Cruz
Watsonville
INSET MAP
Gilroy
Salinas
Monterey

TRAILS AT A GLANCE

NOTE: Open circles indicate that part of the trail is suitable for a given use. See trail description for details.

Trail and/or Park	Distance	Walk	Hike	Run	Kids	Dogs
PACIFICA AND HALF MOON BAY						
1. Milagra Ridge	2.6 miles	●	●	●	○	●
2. Mori Point	2.6 miles	●	●		○	●
3. Sweeney Ridge	6.0 miles	○	●	●	○	●
4. Pedro Point Headlands and Devil's Slide	5.5 miles	○	●	○	○	●
5. Pillar Point Bluff and Mavericks Beach	3.3 miles	●	●	●	●	●
MIDPENINSULA						
6. Sawyer Camp Trail	Up to 7 miles	●	●	●	●	
7. Fifield-Cahill Ridge Trail	Up to 10 miles	●	●		○	
8. Edgewood Park and Natural Preserve	3.5 miles	●	●	●	●	
9. Pulgas Ridge Open Space Preserve	4.1 miles	●	●	●	○	●
10. Huddart Park	4.7 miles		●	●	○	
11. Wunderlich County Park	4.9 miles	●	●	●	○	
SKYLINE BOULEVARD						
12. Purisima Creek Redwoods Preserve	7.3 miles		●	●	○	
13. El Corte de Madera Creek Preserve	5.5 miles	○	●	●	○	
14. Upper La Honda Creek Open Space Preserve	3.9 miles	●	●	●	●	●
15. Windy Hill Open Space Preserve	7.6 miles	○	●	●	○	●

Trail and/or Park	Distance	Walk	Hike	Run	Kids	Dogs
16. Russian Ridge Open Space Preserve	4.9 miles	●	●	●	○	
17. Skyline Ridge Open Space Preserve	4.3 miles	●	●	●	○	
18. Monte Bello Open Space Preserve	6.0 miles		●	●	○	
19. Los Trancos Open Space Preserve	3.1 miles	●	●	●	●	
20. Long Ridge Open Space Preserve	4.6 miles	●	●		○	○
SOUTHERN PENINSULA						
21. Enid W. Pearson-Arastradero Preserve	4.1 miles	●	●	●	●	●
22. Stanford Dish	3.6 miles	●	●	●	○	
23. Foothills Nature Preserve	3.8 miles	●	●	●	○	○
24. Baylands Nature Preserve	5.5 miles	●	●	●	●	●
25. Sunnyvale Bay Trail	5 miles	●	●	●	●	●
26. Rancho San Antonio	5.4 miles	●	●	●	●	
27. Picchetti Ranch Open Space Preserve	4.2 miles	●	●		●	
28. Stevens Creek County Park	2.9 miles	●	●	●	●	●
29. Fremont Older Open Space Preserve	4.5 miles		●	●		●
SARATOGA AND LOS GATOS						
30. Montalvo Arts Center	2.3 miles	○	●		○	●
31. Sanborn County Park	3.4 miles	●	●	●	●	●
32. St. Joseph's Hill Open Space Preserve	3.9 miles	○	●	●	○	●
33. Bear Creek Redwoods Open Space Preserve	5.5 miles	●	●	●	●	
34. Castle Rock State Park	5.7 miles	●	●	●	●	

Trail and/or Park	Distance	Walk	Hike	Run	Kids	Dogs
SAN JOSE AND MILPITAS						
35. Santa Teresa County Park	3.7 miles	○	●	●	○	●
36. Alum Rock Park	6.3 miles	○	●	●	○	
37. Sierra Vista Open Space Preserve	4.6 miles	●	●	●	○	
38. Communications Hill	1.7 miles	●	●	●	●	●
39. Evergreen Urban Hike	2.8 miles	●	●	●	●	●
40. Almaden Quicksilver County Park	6.1 miles	○	●	●	○	●
41. Joseph D. Grant County Park	7.5 miles	○	●	●	○	●
42. Sierra Azul Preserve: Mount Umunhum	8.1 miles	●	●	●	○	
43. Ed R. Levin County Park: Monument Peak	9.3 miles		●		○	●
MORGAN HILL, COYOTE VALLEY, AND GILROY						
44. Calero County Park	5.3 miles	●	●	●	●	●
45. Rancho Cañada del Oro Open Space Preserve	4.2 miles	○	●	●	○	
46. Uvas Canyon County Park	5.1 miles	○	●		○	
47. Coyote Valley Open Space Preserve	4.1 miles	●	●	●	○	
48. Coyote Lake–Harvey Bear Ranch County Park	3.9 miles	●	●	●	●	●
49. Máyyan 'Ooyákma–Coyote Ridge Open Space Preserve	5.2 miles	●	●	●	●	
50. Henry W. Coe State Park	5.3 miles	●	●	●	●	

Next page: Large trees line the trail in the Skyline Ridge Open Space Preserve (Hike 17).

INTRODUCTION

WITH VAST NATURAL AREAS AND a pleasant year-round climate, the San Francisco Peninsula and South Bay are a paradise for hikers. San Mateo and Santa Clara Counties are home to some 2.6 million people, so it may come as a surprise that there is also so much untouched open space here. A quick glance at any map will show you just how much of this area is undeveloped, and on this land you'll find a variety of environments, including chaparral, grasslands, marshlands, oak woodlands, redwoods, and more. Here, just miles outside multiple populous downtowns, you can find yourself walking along the ocean or the Bay, hiking through dense forests, or climbing to hilltops that look out over the whole region.

San Jose is this area's population center, so I've designed this guide to include fifty routes within a one-hour drive of here (with many routes accessible by public transportation too). There are a number of hikes right in San Jose, as well as nearby trails that are important to a given city or town, such as Stevens Creek County Park in Cupertino and St. Joseph's Hill in Los Gatos. You'll hike some waterfront trails, both on the Bay and the ocean, and you'll explore significant county and state parks, such as Joseph D. Grant County Park and Henry W. Coe State Park.

Perhaps one of the most remarkable aspects of this region is all of the work locals have put into land conservation. Two of the parties responsible for saving much of the land you'll explore in this book are the Peninsula Open Space Trust (POST) and the

Santa Clara Valley Open Space Authority. POST raises money to buy land across the Peninsula and South Bay, and then they transfer it to organizations like the Midpeninsula Regional Open Space District for ongoing stewardship. So far they have protected 82,000 acres. The Santa Clara Valley Open Space Authority conserves land in Campbell, Milpitas, Morgan Hill, San Jose, Santa Clara, and unincorporated areas of Santa Clara County. They manage several preserves you can hike in this book, including Coyote Valley Open Space Preserve (Hike 47), Máyyan 'Ooyákma–Coyote Ridge Open Space Preserve (Hike 49), Rancho Cañada del Oro Open Space Preserve (Hike 45), and Sierra Vista Open Space Preserve (Hike 37). To date they have protected around 30,000 acres.

But these organizations aren't alone in their mission. Other cities, counties, regional organizations, and nonprofits (such as the San Francisco Bay Trail Project and the Bay Area Ridge Trail Council) are working tirelessly to open up new land and trails for people in the Bay Area to enjoy.

No matter where you live or what you want to explore—native oak woodlands, tranquil redwoods, grasslands with panoramic views, bayside marshes, or oceanside cliffs—this region has it all. And I hope you'll use this book as your go-to guide and reliable companion for discovering the beauty and variety of this special part of the Bay Area.

CLIMATE AND WEATHER

As mentioned previously, the Peninsula and South Bay known for their great hiking weather, but there are some seasonal patterns to be aware of.

Winter is the area's rainy season, and trails can be muddy. This can range from a mild, slippery annoyance to a thick, sticky muck that is hard to navigate. Temperatures also drop in winter, and hikes—especially those with higher elevations—can get quite cool, so come prepared with appropriate clothing. It also gets dark early in the depths of winter, and completing longer routes in daylight may be challenging. Two hikes that are best in winter are Uvas Canyon County Park (Hike 46) and Los Trancos Open Space Preserve (Hike 19). The six waterfalls in Uvas Canyon come to life after good rainfall, and Los Trancos's streams and waterfalls go from nonexistent in summer to positively flowing in wetter weather.

Spring is the best time to hike across the region. The rain begins to taper off, but the grasslands you see in many of the area's parks are still lush and green from the moisture they received in winter. While exact timing can vary from year to year, grasslands can stay green until mid-May. In this prime season, wildflowers also paint the region's parks and open spaces with a rainbow of color (check out Appendix I to see the best routes for wildflowers). Temperatures are ideal for hiking—not too hot, not too cold. And daylight saving time brings longer days, which means it's prime time to start hiking longer routes again.

Summer can be challenging for hikers. Visually, you could say the hikes are less scenic at this time because the grasslands have turned brown after months of dry weather. And while rain won't likely impact your plans, summer may be uncomfortably hot and shade sparse. To hike safely, make sure you and your hiking companions (including your dogs) have enough water and sun protection. This is an ideal time to hike shaded redwood routes like Bear Creek Redwoods Open Space Preserve (Hike 33), El Corte de Madera Creek Preserve (Hike 13), Huddart Park (Hike 10), and Wunderlich County Park (Hike 11). You can also head to Pacifica and Half Moon Bay, where the weather will likely be cooler and more comfortable.

Fall can have the same mild weather as spring, but without the wildflowers and green grass. At the start of fall, warm summer-like temperatures linger, so don't forget your water and sun protection. Starting in October, rain returns to the area, bringing green grass and cooler temperatures. When

California poppies bring cheery pops of color in spring.

daylight saving time ends in November, it gets dark early again, so opting for shorter routes will ensure you don't find yourself hiking in the dark.

HISTORY

The San Francisco Bay Area is the ancestral homeland of several Native American tribes that resided in the area for up to ten thousand years. Among these tribes, the primary inhabitants were the Ohlone (formerly known as Costanoans from the Spanish "costeño," meaning "coast dweller"), who lived in San Francisco, throughout the East Bay, along the San Francisco Peninsula, and down to Monterey Bay. The Ohlone were not a single unified group but rather a collection of more than fifty distinct tribes, each with their own village, territory, and dialect of related languages. They lived in harmony with the land, relying on hunting, fishing, and gathering for sustenance, and developed sophisticated knowledge of the local ecology.

The arrival of Spanish colonizers in the late eighteenth century brought devastating consequences to the Ohlone. Assimilation into missions, forced labor, and exposure to European diseases led to a drastic decline in their numbers and the disruption of their traditional ways of life. Despite these hardships, some descendants of these tribes and tribelets remain today and are actively working to preserve and revive their cultures, languages, and traditions, and to advocate for their rights and recognition.

In this book you will wander through Ohlone ancestral lands. You will see references to Ohlone tribes in the writeups for Sweeney Ridge (Aramai, a Ramaytush Ohlone tribelet, Hike 3), Máyyan 'Ooyákma (Muwekma Ohlone Tribe, Hike 49) and Mount Umunhum (Amah Mutsun Ohlone Tribal Band, Hike 42).

FLORA AND FAUNA

While there are several different types of environments across this region, you will see some of the same flora and fauna across the trails of the Peninsula and South Bay. This section talks about some common species to help you identify the plants and animals you might encounter on your hikes.

TREES AND PLANTS

Here are some common trees and plants to look for while you're out exploring.

Coast redwoods are the world's tallest trees. They have fibrous reddish bark, and for their size, they have comparatively small cones. Redwoods don't only reproduce with cones but also with clones. At the base of many redwood trees, you'll see baby redwoods sprouting. Many of the redwoods you'll see on the trails in this book are second-growth trees, meaning they're not the original trees that grew here. The better part of a generation of trees was logged, and this new generation of trees has grown in their place. Some say old-growth redwoods can be as young as 200 years old, but many think that true old-growth redwoods are 500 to 1,000 years old. I mention some notable old-growth redwoods in parks like Bear Creek Redwoods Open Space Preserve (Hike 33) and upper La Honda Creek Open Space Preserve (Hike 14), and in the Go Farther section of El Corte de Madera Open Space Preserve (Hike 13).

Douglas-firs are another giant of Bay Area forests. Their bark is gray-brown as opposed to the cinnamon color of redwood bark. For me, the easiest way to find a Douglas-fir is to look for its cones on the forest floor. The cones are conical with a tapered, pointed tip, and they are generally 2 to 4 inches in length. Distinctive three-pointed bracts (outer cone scales) also protrude from the cones. Other fun facts about Douglas-firs are that they are not firs at all, but rather "false hemlocks," and that they get both their scientific name (*Pseudotsuga menziesii*) and their common name from two Scottish botanists: Archibald Menzies and David Douglas, respectively.

California bay laurels typically grow from 40 to 80 feet and have narrow, oblong, glossy green leaves. It's not necessarily the leaves, however, that will clue you into these trees' presence along the trails. The real surefire identifier of the bay laurel is its intoxicating aroma. Some people call these trees pepperwoods due to the peppery smell of the leaves when crushed. I may be alone in this, but I think they smell like cream soda. And yes, these leaves are related to the dried bay leaves you can cook with, but beware! They are much more potent and can overpower your dishes if you use too big of a leaf in your cooking.

Chaparral is a catch-all term for a variety of low-growing shrubs or other scrub-like plants that line many trails in this region. I use scrub plants and chaparral interchangeably throughout the book.

Oaks are some of the most common trees in California. Three species you'll see across the routes in this book are the coast live oak, the canyon live oak, and the valley oak. The coast live oak is evergreen and ranges from 30 to 80 feet tall. Look for firm, shiny, leathery leaves with spines and acorns. Canyon live oaks are the most widespread oak species in California. They can grow to anywhere between 15 and 100 feet and are often spotted at higher elevations. They are evergreen, with long, flat, and oblong leaves, and their acorns have distinctive, shallow caps. Valley oaks grow between 50 and 100 feet tall. They're deciduous and have larger, more rounded leaves and larger acorns.

Manzanitas and madrones are two types of trees with a distinctive red color. In both trees, their outer bark peels, revealing a smooth red bark underneath. Manzanitas are smaller—from a few feet to 10 to 12 feet tall—and are often found in scrub plant communities. Madrones are much larger than manzanitas, growing from 80 to 120 feet tall.

Poison oak is seen throughout the Bay Area. It contains urushiol, an oil that can cause a skin rash or blisters. Remembering the old adage "leaves of three, let it be" can help you avoid it. To distinguish poison oak from other plants with clusters of three leaves, remember that poison oak leaves have smooth edges, rather than jagged ones, and can be green or red. In winter, when there might not be leaves to help you identify poison oak, stay away from smooth branches; if the plant you're looking at has thorns, it may be blackberry. On official trails, you are unlikely to come into direct contact with poison oak. If you think you or your pet has been exposed, wash your clothes, yourself, and your pet. Products like Tecnu can remove poison oak oil from your skin in case of exposure, but soap and water also get the job done.

Toyons are also known as Christmas berry or California holly. Just like traditional holly leaves, toyon leaves have jagged edges. In summer, you can spot toyons by their white flowers. And in winter, they feature clusters of deep red berries. The berries of the tree are edible only when dried or

Fields of colorful wildflowers greet hikers in the springtime.

cooked, as the raw berries contain cyanide. The Ohlone made a tea from toyon leaves and flowers as a treatment for upset stomach and menstrual pain.

WILDFLOWERS

There are hundreds of wildflower species in the 75 or so miles between Pacifica and Gilroy. The peak time to view wildflowers may vary according to the microclimate of the area you're in, but viewing is generally best in springtime, with a peak between mid-March and mid-May. Here is a sampling of just some of the native wildflowers you may see along the trail.

California poppies are the iconic wildflower of this region—and of California as a whole, being named the state flower in 1903. Their cheery orange color brightens up hillsides in spring and summer. They have four petals, grow well in full sun, and close at night.

Paintbrushes come in red, orange, and yellow and grow on hillsides and mountains. There is also a coastal variety called coast paintbrush. These flowers are "hemi-parasites," meaning they get some of their nutrients from a host plant. They also rely on pollinators to reproduce.

Mariposa lilies grow from bulbs and thrive in rock outcrops and serpentine soil often inhospitable to other flowers. The seventy or so flowers with this name have similar appearances but come in a variety of colors. They are called "mariposa" (Spanish for "butterfly") lilies, as their delicate petals are reminiscent of a butterfly's wings when they blow in the wind.

Lupines are a member of the pea family and they flower in many colors, but they are most commonly purple. They appear in grasslands in springtime and feature tall, tapered columns of flowers.

Tidy tips are tiny members of the sunflower family. These daisy-like blooms have yellow centers with a "tidy" transition to their white tips. They're an important food source for insects and butterflies, including the endangered Bay checkerspot butterfly. They can be found in chapparal and grassland environments, but they thrive best on the coast.

Trilliums are often spotted on the forest floor, and their three-petaled blooms can be white, pink, or a deep red.

Common yarrow grows throughout California. It has long stalks with fern-like leaves and flat-topped clusters of small flowers. It blooms in several colors but is most commonly white. Yarrow can easily be confused with Queen Anne's lace, which also grows in the Bay Area.

To learn more about the many other varieties of local wildflowers and which ones are in which parks, visit the respective park and land manager websites. And to see which hikes are best for wildflowers, see Appendix I.

WILDLIFE

The Peninsula and South Bay are thriving habitats for animals, both big and small. Here are some of the local wildlife species to keep an eye out for.

Banana slugs and the redwood forest go hand in hand. In these environments, banana slugs play a key role: helping matter decompose—anything from dead plants to animal droppings and more. Their bright yellow color makes them easy to spot, and they sometimes have brown spots, just like their namesake fruit. Banana slugs are the largest land slug in North America and can grow up to almost 10 inches in length.

Bay checkerspot butterflies have a checkered pattern of white, black, and reddish-orange markings and live throughout the serpentine grasslands of San Mateo and Santa Clara Counties. They became a threatened species in 1987, and as of 2022, they are considered endangered. Like many butterflies, the Bay checkerspot is short-lived, with an average lifespan of ten days. The best time to keep an eye out for these elusive creatures is between late February and early May. They look similar to more common species, like the field crescent and northern crescent, so you may want to use a mobile identification app to confirm a spotting.

Bobcats, named for their short, bobbed tails, range between 17 and 25 pounds: roughly two to three times the size of a house cat and a quarter the size of a mountain lion. Bobcats are wary of people, so they aren't thought to pose much of a threat to humans, but they are more likely to attack pets. To keep bobcats afraid of humans, you can use negative conditioning by "hazing" them. This means making yourself look scary by raising your arms above your head, yelling, or making loud noises in their vicinity. When I was hiking in Sanborn County Park in 2023, a ranger told me that a bobcat family lived not far from that park's Sequoia parking lot.

Coyotes roam throughout the parks featured in this book. They are generally nocturnal but can be active in the early morning and at sunset. You're less likely to see a coyote in the middle of the day, but if you do see one, it doesn't mean it's sick. Keep your dog on leash or under voice command, never feed coyotes, and do not turn your back on them or run. Coyote attacks on people are very rare, so there's no need to be afraid. But if one approaches you, shout at it or throw small rocks in its direction (not directly at it).

Cows are used to grazing grasslands in area parks. Grazing, which often takes places during the winter and early spring, reduces fire risk and encourages native plants and wildlife to thrive. You'll want to be especially mindful of cows when they have calves with them, as they may charge you if they think their babies are threatened. I have been charged by cows in Ed R. Levin County Park, and it was quite frightening!

Mountain lions live in many Bay Area parks; in fact, you'll often see informative (and intimidating) signs at trailheads warning of their presence. But don't let that scare you! Here are a few facts to keep you calm. Mountain lions are nocturnal, so it's unlikely you'd encounter them during daytime hikes. Attacks on humans are also extremely rare. If you encounter a mountain lion, the California Department of Fish and Wildlife recommends making yourself look large, standing tall, and maintaining eye contact. Slowly back away while facing the animal. Do not run, crouch down, or turn your back on it. If it offers some comfort, I have hiked all over the Bay Area and have yet to see a mountain lion.

Ticks live close to the ground in areas with tall grass, brush, and trees. I recommend doing a full-body tick check

Tule elk are known to roam around the trails of Máyyan 'Ooyákma—Coyote Ridge Open Space Preserve (Hike 49). (Photo: David Mauk)

after each hike. If you find a tick on your body, remove it with tweezers (making sure you get the head) and put it in a jar or plastic bag that you can keep in the freezer for later identification if necessary. Wash the affected area with warm water and soap and monitor bites for any suspicious changes in appearance.

Rattlesnakes are an uncommon sight, but it's still possible you might spot one—especially in warmer months when snakes are more active. I have personally seen a rattlesnake in Ed R. Levin County Park, right in a parking lot! Paying close attention to your surroundings can help you identify rattlesnakes. Try to look at the ground ahead of you as you walk, look carefully around logs and rocks before sitting down, and avoid putting your hands or feet in places where you can't see clearly. If you encounter a rattlesnake, keep your distance, and if you can't go around it, turn around and walk the other way. Stay on marked trails and avoid brush where they may be hiding, noting that this message applies to your furry friends too. If you or your pet are bitten, stay calm and call 911 as soon as possible.

Tule elk are a species of elk found only in California. They were once hunted almost to extinction but have now made a resurgence due to conservation efforts. They are known to be plentiful around Point Reyes in Marin County, and you can also find them in the South Bay, including in the serpentine grasslands of Máyyan 'Ooyákma–Coyote Ridge Open Space Preserve (Hike 49), Joseph D. Grant County Park (Hike 41), and Coyote Lake–Harvey Bear Ranch County Park (Hike 48). To increase your chances of viewing elk, look for them in the cooler months and earlier in the day, but be sure to maintain your distance so as not to disturb them—the National Park Service recommends staying at least 75 feet away, or about two school bus lengths.

Pigs were brought to California by Spanish and Russian settlers in the 1700s as livestock. Those that escaped became feral and are now considered wild pigs. Steer clear of these animals if you spot them; give them space so they can escape and make noise to scare them off. I've seen wild pigs in Joseph D. Grant County Park (Hike 41).

NOTABLE REGIONAL MOUNTAINS

You will see several of the same mountains time and time again on these hikes. While some of the Bay Area mountains are harder to recognize just by their shape, a few have distinctive features. I like to use the PeakFinder mobile app to identify mountains. Hold up your phone to a distant mountain range and see a silhouette of that range along with mountain names and elevations.

Mount Diablo is part of the eponymous Diablo Range in the East Bay. From many angles, Mount Diablo looks like it has two summits: its principal summit (3,849 feet) and North Peak (3,557 feet), which is about 1 mile northeast of the main summit. From some angles, however, you'll only see the main summit. Mount Diablo is found much farther north than other Diablo Range mountains, such as Mission Peak, Mount Allison, and Monument Peak. Two hikes on Mount Diablo are featured in *Urban Trails: East Bay*.

Mission Peak, Mount Allison, and Monument Peak are three Diablo Range peaks that start about 25 miles south of Mount Diablo as the crow flies. If you're looking at these peaks from the west, they appear as if they're sitting in a row. From north to south, you'll see Mission Peak (2,516 feet), then Mount Allison (2,664 feet), then Monument Peak (2,594 feet). From afar, you won't see any towers on Mission Peak's summit, but there are a number of them on Mount Allison's summit and a few on Monument Peak's summit.

Mount Hamilton (4,265 feet) is in the Diablo Range 40 miles southeast of Mount Diablo as the crow flies. It is identifiable by the white domed buildings at its summit. This is the Lick Observatory, an astronomical observatory owned and operated by the University of California. There is no public hiking trail to the top of this peak.

Mount Umunhum (3,489 feet) is the fourth-tallest peak in the Santa Cruz Mountains after Loma Prieta, Crystal Peak, and Mount Chual. At its summit, there's a large rectangular building: the base of a radar dish, once part of the Almaden Air Force Station. You can climb to the top of Mount Umunhum following Hike 42 in this book.

Loma Prieta (3,786 feet) is easy to spot south of Mount Umunhum in the Santa Cruz Mountains. There is a collection of communication towers at its summit. You can hike to the top of Loma Prieta, but the mountain is located too far outside our one-hour radius of San Jose to include in this book.

LOOKING BACK ON THE TWO years when I researched, planned, and hiked all of these routes, I am in awe of the places I have been and what I have seen and learned. A contented smile spreads across my face as beautiful images and memories flash before my eyes. While I will surely continue to revisit the parks and open spaces featured in this book, now it's your turn, so get out there and explore! I hope you will appreciate this special corner of the Bay Area as much as I do. Feel free to reach out to me with your experiences and thoughts at alexandra@urbanhikersf.com.

HOW TO USE THIS GUIDE

EACH HIKE DESCRIBED IN THIS book includes information to help you decide if the route is right for you and your hiking companions. I have personally hiked every trail in this book (often many times!) and have had hike testers follow in my footsteps to make sure the directions are accurate and up to date as of the time of writing. Trails open and close and routes can change, however, so make sure you research each park's current trail maps, conditions, alerts, and closures before you go.

THE DESTINATIONS

This book is divided into seven sections and is organized from north to south, but you can choose how you want to explore. You can select a particular area to get acquainted with, or you can head to Appendix I to choose a trail by distance, type of scenery, elevation gain, or difficulty.

Here is a quick overview of the areas featured in this book:

When the Peninsula and the South Bay are scorching and dry in summer, the coastal hikes of Pacifica and Half Moon Bay bring cool relief. Further down the Peninsula and moving inland, the Midpeninsula region, including the cities of San Mateo and Redwood City, offers easily accessible ways to immerse yourself in nature. Continuing further south and heading west, discover wilder, more remote hikes along the Skyline Boulevard/State Route 35 Corridor. This area features redwoods and grasslands with views of the Peninsula, Santa Clara Valley, Santa Cruz Mountains, and the ocean.

The hikes of the Southern Peninsula hop back east from those in the Skyline Boulevard/State Route 35 Corridor section. Just like the Midpeninsula, these routes are all near major cities, but this time you're hiking in Santa Clara County in places like Cupertino, Los Altos, Palo Alto, Portola Valley, and Sunnyvale. Next up, I've chosen five hikes in Los Gatos and Saratoga. These routes mix town and country, so you'll hike on serene trails in otherwise developed areas and take wilder routes through dense forests of redwoods and Douglas-firs with occasional ocean and mountain views.

The next section is all about hikes in and around San Jose, with one in Milpitas. Here you'll find a few urban hiking routes as well as several with a backwoods feel, including the two longest ones in the book. For more San Jose hiking, be sure to check out Appendix II. This is a list of straightforward trails that don't require directions but may be a fun source of extra hiking inspiration. The last section in the book is the southernmost region, highlighting trails in Morgan Hill, the Coyote Valley, and Gilroy. Here you find yourself in horse country, where San Francisco and San Jose feel a world away.

No matter where you're hiking and which route you choose, I aim to orient you in a similar way. Here's what to look for at the start of each write-up:

Distance: This is the length of the hike in miles. Unless otherwise noted, all distances listed are roundtrip. I used a GPS watch to measure all distances for these hikes.

Elevation Gain: Most routes include both ascents and descents, but this number gives you an overall picture of how much you'll be climbing. I used a GPS watch to measure the elevation gain for these hikes.

High Point: This is the highest elevation on a given hike. A big high point isn't always correlated with a difficult hike. It can mean that a route has a lot of elevation gain, but it can also just mean that a route starts high up to begin with. Make sure to look at distance, elevation gain, high point, and difficulty to get a good sense of whether a hike is a good fit for you.

Difficulty: Hikes in this book are rated easy, moderate, challenging, or difficult. The ratings are based on trail surfaces and conditions, distance, and elevation gain. About a quarter of the routes are easy, half are moderate, and about a quarter are challenging, with a few difficult ones. The hilly terrain in this region weighted the hikes slightly more toward moderate and challenging, but rest assured that there are some shorter options and even accessible trails on many of the longer routes. Be sure to check out each hike's write-up to see if there's a Make It Shorter option if you need it.

Time: This is how long it took me to hike a given route. My estimated times are for continuous hiking and do not include breaks at overlooks or picnic areas. Though I hike a lot, I am not a speed hiker; however, you may want to allocate additional time for snacks, views, and other stops.

Fitness: Each description mentions whether walkers, hikers, or runners might like the route. I've based my rationale on the assumption that walkers would probably like all the routes rated easy plus some of the longer ones on well-maintained trails. I assumed runners wouldn't like the steep trails, and I assumed hikers would like all of the trails! Of course, you are free to hike, walk, or run (except when running is prohibited) on any of the trails in this book.

Family-Friendly: I note whether a given route is family-friendly as-is, and I also note ways to make longer and more challenging routes family-friendly when possible. While I offer ideas and suggestions, parents are the best judges of whether their children are capable of completing a given route.

Dog-Friendly: While many parks on the Peninsula don't allow dogs, I am a huge dog lover and tried to maximize the dog-friendly trails in this book! The information you see here

Many trails have helpful signposts to guide you. As for dog poop bags, please carry them with you and dispose of them properly.

is based on the regulations for each trail and natural area. If dogs are allowed, I have listed whether they need to be on leash. If an area allows dogs off leash, be sure to keep your dog under voice command and always bring water for them and clean up after them. Bagging up poop but leaving it alongside the trail to pick up later does not count as cleaning up after your dog!

Amenities: These include restrooms, benches, picnic areas, historic sights, scenic overlooks, visitor centers, and more.

Contact: This is the organization or group that manages the land the trail passes through. See Appendix III for contact information, including websites and phone numbers.

Before You Go: This includes any additional information that you may find useful before setting off on your hike.

GPS: GPS coordinates for the trailhead (in degrees, minutes, and seconds) are provided for each hike.

Maps: A detailed map shows the trailhead, the route, points of interest, and amenities.

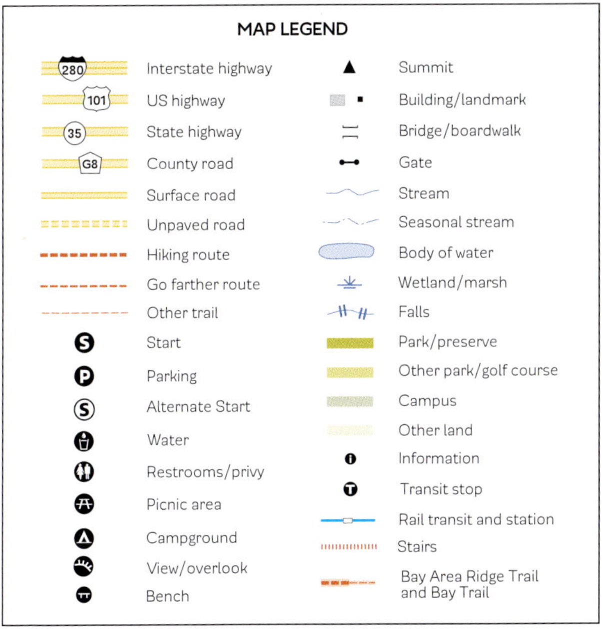

After the Getting There header, you'll see the following information:

Map to: This is the address you should enter in your preferred map app. I have verified that all of these addresses work for Google Maps; however, they may not work in all map apps.

Public Transit: Public transit routes are listed when available. If you don't see any public transit information associated with a given hike, that means there's no good option.

Parking: I provide parking information and any fees for parking, if applicable. Parking is free unless otherwise noted.

Moving on from the headers, each destination also features an overview that showcases hike highlights or area history to help you get excited about a given route.

Below the hike overview, you'll also find two additional sections:

Get Moving: This section provides the directions to follow (along with the map) and the sites you will see on your route.

Go Farther or Make it Shorter: This section includes ways that you can extend the hike or make it easier or shorter. In a few instances, it also highlights places you may want to visit after the hike.

PERMITS, REGULATIONS, AND PARK FEES

Most of the hikes in this book are operated and maintained by open space managers, regional trail systems, or various counties or cities. While many parks do not charge an entrance fee, some do charge parking fees. One hike in this book requires an entry permit (Hike 14), one requires a parking permit (Hike 46), and one is docent-led only (Hike 7).

For all routes, refer to each individual hike write-up to determine whether permits are required, if dogs are allowed, and if there are fees for cars or dogs. Fees and regulations can occasionally change, so it's always a good idea to double-check with local agencies before you hit the trails.

ROAD AND TRAIL CONDITIONS

New trails are added to parks from time to time, and some trails in this book are affected by seasonal closures in wet weather or other conditions, such as fallen trees, erosion, and washouts. Please refer to park websites (see Appendix III) to ensure the trails you want to visit are open. Another option is to visit websites like alltrails.com to read recent trail reports and see if hikers have encountered trails that were muddy, impassable, or otherwise unpleasant.

OUTDOOR ETHICS

At the core of outdoor ethics is the principle of Leave No Trace (LNT), which means that you should leave the trail (and park) as good as or better than you found it. If you bring something into a park, pack it out. And if you find litter on the trail, pack that out too.

The Leave No Trace Center for Outdoor Ethics "protects the outdoors by teaching and inspiring people to enjoy it responsibly." Their seven LNT principles help people reduce their impact on natural areas:

1. Plan ahead and prepare.
2. Travel and camp on durable surfaces.
3. Dispose of waste properly.
4. Leave what you find.
5. Minimize campfire impacts.
6. Respect wildlife.
7. Be considerate of others.

And while some of these principles apply more to overnight trips, it is helpful for outdoor enthusiasts to be familiar with and follow them. Learn more at lnt.org/why/7-principles.

TRAIL ETIQUETTE

Observing proper hiking etiquette keeps you safe while hiking and also ensures that future generations can enjoy trails, parks, and natural areas. Here are some general guidelines:

- **Obey park rules.** This one is pretty simple. If a park isn't open to dogs, keep your pup at home. If bicycles are not allowed on a trail, don't bring your bike. If you find yourself with a bike on a trail that prohibits bikes, walk while pushing your bike instead of riding it.
- **Stay on trails.** Don't take shortcuts or unofficial trails that cause erosion or harm sensitive environments.
- **Observe the right-of-way.** When you encounter cyclists or horseback riders, move to the side of the trail and let them pass. Hikers are more nimble and able to move off the trail.
- **Keep dogs under control.** Trail users should follow dog regulations at all times. Dogs should be on leash or under very strict voice command. If leashes are required, please

use a leash no matter how friendly your pup is; some people and dogs are uncomfortable around unfamiliar dogs. And always pack out your dog's poop and discard it properly. Do not leave it alongside the trail to pick up later.

- **Halt for horses.** As mentioned above, when you see a horseback rider, step to the side of the trail. You don't want to catch a horse off guard. Make yourself visible so the horse sees you but also crouch down to make yourself look smaller. If you encounter a horse on a slope, try to step downhill of it; if spooked, horses tend to run uphill, and you don't want to be in the way should that happen. Don't raise your voice around a horse, although talking calmly to its rider can help reassure the horse that you don't pose a threat.
- **Leave wildlife alone.** Giving wildlife a wide berth can keep you and wild animals safe. Don't roll rocks off cliffs. You never know who or what is below you, and falling rocks can cause serious injuries.
- **Don't bring home things you find in a park.** Don't bring sticks, rocks, shells, or other natural features home with you. Leave them where you find them. It's fine to inspect things you discover, especially with curious kids, but don't remove them from their natural environment.
- **Leave no trace.** If you bring something on a trail, pack it out with you. This practice helps keep the trail in good condition for future hikers.

WATER AND GEAR

While most of the trails in this book can be enjoyed without much preparation or gear, it's always a good idea to bring water, even if you're just out for a quick walk or run. Water is essential for hydration and can also be used to clean out scrapes or cuts.

In terms of gear, you will want to make sure you have good walking or hiking shoes. Walking around in flip-flops or other loose, open-toed shoes can lead to tripping and can make it easier to injure your feet. Shoes aren't the only thing to evaluate carefully when you prepare for a hike. See the Ten Essentials below for a full list of gear that can help you stay safe on any hike.

THE TEN ESSENTIALS

It's always good to know you have the Ten Essentials (developed by The Mountaineers) in case of an emergency.

Navigation: Stay on track by using the maps in this book as well as park maps or a smartphone app. If you're relying on your phone, even if you may think you'll have cell service for your entire hike, it's always a good idea to download maps that you can use when offline in case you end up without coverage. Some apps like Gaia GPS rely on a GPS signal, which you may still have, especially on open ridges or summits, even when you do not have a cell signal.

Headlamp: In winter the days are shorter, which makes a headlamp or flashlight handy, but even in summer, you may find yourself on the trail as the sun sets. A headlamp takes up very little room in your backpack and can help you stay safe if you end up hiking after dark.

Wide-brimmed sun hats are a great choice for hikers, especially for trails with little tree cover (Hike 43).

A NOTE ABOUT SAFETY

Safety is an important concern in all outdoor activities. No guidebook can alert you to every hazard or anticipate the limitations of every reader. Therefore, the descriptions of roads, trails, routes, and natural features in this book are not representations that a particular place or excursion will be safe for your party. When you follow any of the routes described in this book, you assume responsibility for your own safety. Under normal conditions, such excursions require the usual attention to traffic, road and trail conditions, weather, terrain, the capabilities of your party, and other factors. Keeping informed on current conditions and exercising common sense are the keys to a safe, enjoyable outing.

—Mountaineers Books

Sun protection: The Peninsula and South Bay can be a very sunny place; it's always best to be prepared for the sun with sunglasses, sunscreen, and a good hat. Some outdoor clothing comes with built-in sun protection.

First-aid supplies: Trips, falls, and other accidents can happen to anyone at any time. Be prepared for the unexpected by carrying a small first-aid kit with items such as band-aids, gauze, antiseptic cream, and an elastic bandage for ankle sprains. If you have allergies that require medication, particularly to bees, bring your EpiPen or other personal medication. And make sure your hiking buddies know about your allergies and medications. A little prep can go a long way!

Knife: Tools (like a knife and a multitool) can help you do anything from opening a food bag to removing a splinter to cutting cloth into bandages.

Fire: It is extremely unlikely that you'll unintentionally spend the night out on the trails described in this guide, but in case this happens, you may want to carry matches in a waterproof bag or a lighter to start a fire in an emergency.

Shelter: In an emergency, a rain poncho or garbage bag can serve as a temporary shelter. If you want to bring along an ultralight tent, some of them can weigh as little as two pounds.

Extra food: Food is fuel. Make sure you have enough for your hike. If you bring extra, you can extend your hike or feed unprepared friends.

Extra water: Access to potable water on trails can be spotty, so make sure you bring all you need and more on your hike. If you're using water from natural sources, such as creeks, you'll also want a way to purify your water, either with a filter or through a chemical or other sterilization method.

Extra clothes: Layering is essential in this region, where the temperature can be very different in the sun versus the shade and during the day versus at night. Depending on what the weather forecast looks like, you may want to bring extra clothing, like wool arm warmers, a long-sleeved shirt, a coat (rain jacket or windbreaker as well as a fleece or other insulating layer), a hat, a scarf, and gloves.

TRAIL CONCERNS

Trails and parks are generally safe places for recreation, but it's always a good idea to be aware of your surroundings—especially if you're on the trail by yourself. It's also a good idea to share your hiking plans with a reliable friend or family member, including when you're heading out and what route you'll be taking.

Car break-ins are unfortunate but do happen from time to time at trail parking lots. When you bring a car to a park, never leave anything of value, like a wallet or cell phone, in the car. It's also a good idea to move any bags from the car seats to the trunk. Thieves don't know that a bag is empty. Don't tempt their curiosity.

After you've read this introduction, you're ready to hit the trails. Without further ado, here we go!

Next page: View toward Mori Point from the Mori Peak Trail (Hike 2)

PACIFICA AND HALF MOON BAY

Pacifica and Half Moon Bay are the Bay Area's natural air conditioners. When they're not socked in with fog, these charming coastal cities offer expansive views over the sparkling Pacific. They're also an escape when the rest of the Bay Area heats up in summer. In this chapter, you'll hike Milagra Ridge, where you'll walk around an old gun battery and explore a ridge with scenic ocean views. Mori Point brings out the crowds, and you'll visit an overlook and climb Mori Peak at this popular oceanside park. Next, you'll head to the top of Sweeney Ridge and learn the complex history of the Portolá Discovery Site. The Pedro Point Headlands and Devil's Slide route gives you two hikes in one. In the Pedro Point Headlands, you'll climb forested trails to reach cliffside bluffs high over the ocean. Then you'll explore old Highway 1 on the paved, accessible Devil's Slide trail. Lastly, you'll head to Half Moon Bay's scenic Pillar Point Bluff to take in panoramic views from sandy trails. At the end of this route, you'll head to Mavericks Beach, which is home to world-famous surf competitions. As a bonus, all of these hikes are dog-friendly! Make sure to hike on sunny days to make the most of the ocean views.

1 Milagra Ridge

DISTANCE:	2.6 miles
ELEVATION GAIN:	600 feet
HIGH POINT:	710 feet
DIFFICULTY:	Moderate
TIME:	1 hour and 30 minutes
FITNESS:	Hikers, walkers, runners
FAMILY-FRIENDLY:	Families can see Make It Shorter.
DOG-FRIENDLY:	Yes, on leash
AMENITIES:	Restrooms, benches
CONTACT:	Golden Gate National Recreation Area
GPS:	37° 38' 35.5236" N, 122° S29' 19.8672" W

GETTING THERE

Map to: Milagra Overlook Hiking Trail. **Public Transit:** Take SamTrans bus 110 to Oceana Boulevard and Milagra Drive or bus 112 to 700 Palmetto Avenue - SF RV Resort. From there, it's a 0.3- or 0.5-mile walk to the start. **Parking:** Free parking. The lot at the end of Connemara Drive has eight standard spaces and one ADA space.

"Milagra Ridge" means "miracle ridge," and the scenery here is indeed divine. You'll quickly climb into nature on the Milagra Battery and Summit Trails, where you'll sometimes encounter a stone labyrinth and always get sweeping ocean views—as long as Karl the Fog stays away, that is. As you walk, think of this area's rich history and people, including the Ohlone, who were the original inhabitants; the Spanish, who farmed here in the 1700s; and the US Army, which installed a gun battery in the 1940s, and later, a Nike missile site. The land ultimately became part of the Golden Gate National Recreation Area in 1987, and most of the route is on the Bay Area Ridge Trail.

A labyrinth is sometimes (but not always) seen along the Milagra Battery Trail.

GET MOVING

Pick up the Milagra Battery Trail from the back of the parking lot on Connemara Drive. Almost immediately, you pass an overlook with an ocean view as you start to follow the switchbacks uphill on a wide dirt trail lined by grasses, coyote brush, yarrow, California sagebrush, and mustard. Ignore any turnoffs from the main trail.

At an overlook and bench at 0.4 mile, look south to Mori Point, Sharp Park Beach, and Montara Mountain's North Peak.

Shortly thereafter, reach a wide-open area to your left where there is sometimes a hand-crafted stone labyrinth. At 0.6 mile, reach Battery 244, a World War II–era bunker, where a short trail leads to an overlook with a view of the ocean (not included in route mileage).

You're now on paved Milagra Ridge Road, but not for long. Where the road splits, climb a stairway on your left, picking up the Milagra Summit Trail. From the top, take in 360-degree views of the ocean and San Bruno Mountain to the northeast. When you're done soaking in the scene, continue on the trail, then head left down a stairway to reach Milagra Ridge Road once again, passing the Milagra Creek Overlook Trail just before this.

Turn left at the paved road and enjoy a flat stretch. At 1 mile, you arrive at the only restroom on the route. After the restroom, stay left on the wide paved road. Ignore an almost immediate turnoff for the Milagra Spur Trail on your right and continue to the end of Milagra Ridge Road at 1.3 miles. Toward the end of this stretch, pass a North Coast County Water District reservoir.

At the end of the trail, pass through a yellow gate and almost immediately pick up stairs for the Milagra Ridge Trail on the right. This narrow dirt trail climbs through chaparral to 710 feet, the highest point on this route. Gaze at the Pacific as you walk along the ridge, then head down a stairway and reach the other end of the Milagra Spur Trail.

Continue straight on the Milagra Ridge Trail, then follow the path as it winds around to a T at 1.7 miles. Turn left and enjoy a stretch with especially stunning ocean views. This trail dead-ends into paved Milagra Ridge Road at 2 miles, where you pass the Milagra Summit stairs on your right. From here, retrace your steps for 0.6 mile back to the parking lot.

MAKE IT SHORTER

Families, walkers, and beginner hikers may want to turn around at Battery 244, 0.6 mile into the route.

2 Mori Point

DISTANCE: 2.6 miles
ELEVATION GAIN: 420 feet
HIGH POINT: 330 feet
DIFFICULTY: Easy to challenging
TIME: 1 hour and 15 minutes
FITNESS: Hikers, walkers
FAMILY-FRIENDLY: Yes, see Make It Shorter
DOG-FRIENDLY: Yes, on leash
AMENITIES: Restrooms, benches, accessible trails
CONTACT: Golden Gate National Recreation Area
BEFORE YOU GO: Bring hiking poles for the main route detailed here.
GPS: 37° 37' 6.7944" N, 122° 29' 8.7576" W

GETTING THERE

Map to: Mori Point Road and Bradford Way, Pacifica. **Public Transit:** Take SamTrans Bus 110 to the Highway 1 and Westport Drive stop. From here, walk 0.2 mile to the hike start. **Parking:** Free parking. There are just a few spaces in the lot, and they can fill up quickly. Luckily, local streets allow for parking.

Mori Point is a small place with big views: Its 110 acres form a promontory above the sparkling Pacific looking north to Point Reyes and south to Pedro Point. If you can handle the 200 or so steps on this route, you'll have one of the shortest hikes to the best views of the ocean in this book. Plus, if you time your hike just right, Mori Point also hosts one of the area's best wildflower displays, with tidy tips and goldfields forming a carpet of yellow at the point itself. The best time to view wildflowers at Mori Point is in April.

Mori Point was once a limestone quarry. In 1889, Italian immigrant Stefano Mori purchased 19 acres here for farming and ranching. His twenty-one-room farmhouse later became

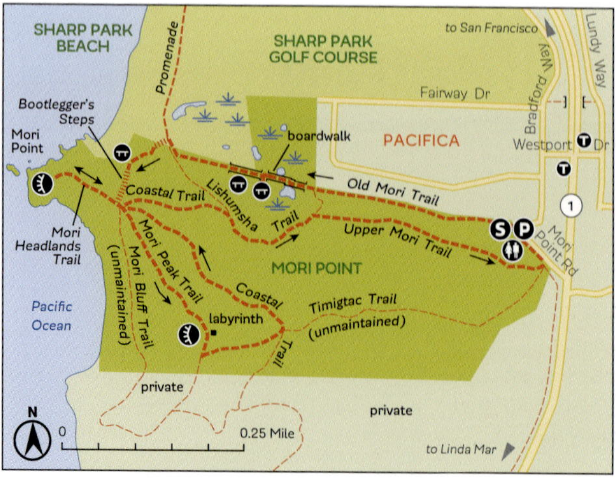

The 185 or so Bootlegger's Steps give you views of Sharp Park Beach as you head up to Mori Point.

the Mori Point Inn—an inn, yes, but also a site for smuggling Canadian whiskey into the United States (hence the route's "Bootlegger's Steps"). The inn remained open until 1965 but burned down in 1966. Today Mori Point is owned by the Golden Gate National Recreation Area.

Note: This route has a steep ascent and stairs. If you're not up for that, see Make It Shorter for two options that suit a broader range of ability levels.

GET MOVING

From the parking lot, pick up the Old Mori Trail, a wide, flat, and accessible dirt trail. Fences line the right side of the trail, delineating the area from a Pacifica neighborhood. After 0.3 mile, the dirt trail turns into a boardwalk for a bit. (Ignore turn-offs on the left and right before the start of the boardwalk.) From here, you can look left and see two peaks. The one farther west is Mori Peak, and you'll climb it later on this route.

At a junction at 0.5 mile, head left and climb a small flight of stairs and then turn right to follow the trail uphill. After a few hundred feet, you reach the bottom of the Bootlegger's Steps, around 185 steps that lead to a junction of five trails. From the top of the steps, enjoy northward views toward the ocean and Sharp Park Beach, then turn right and walk a short distance to reach Mori Point. After exploring the point, return to the top of the Bootlegger's Steps.

Of the four trails in front of you, take the second one from the right, the Mori Peak Trail (no trail sign). Pass some concrete barriers on your left after 375 feet and head uphill toward Mori Peak. The trail is steep, so please proceed with caution. If you have hiking poles, you'll want to use them here.

Climb 0.1 mile to the top of Mori Peak to enjoy this view over the ocean. At times, a hand-crafted stone labyrinth greets you at the summit. Here, head right and turn left in 100 feet onto the narrow Timigtac Trail (no trail sign).

When you reach the bottom of Mori Peak, another hill is in front of you; instead of climbing it, turn left on the Coastal Trail (no trail sign). After 0.2 mile, arrive at a clearing and continue a bit farther toward the now familiar intersection at the Bootlegger's Steps. Just before reaching the steps, take a right on the Coastal Trail toward the Lishumsha Trail. Stay on the Coastal Trail, a wide fire road, for 0.2 mile. Then continue straight as is merges with the Lishumsha Trail. When the trail splits after 725 feet, stay right to pick up the Upper Mori Trail. Continue for 0.3 mile until the trail lets out onto Mori Point Road. Turn left (walking carefully as there is no sidewalk here) to reach the parking lot after a brief walk.

GO FARTHER

Explore the waterside Mori Bluff Trail, but be careful, as this trail is unmaintained. You can also head to the Calera Creek Trail across Highway 1 from Reina Del Mar Avenue. Along this accessible trail, Irish immigrant and longtime Pacifica resident Mike Mooney installed his "Liberty Gardens" here in 2001 as a tribute to those lost on 9/11.

MAKE IT SHORTER

For the easiest option, at the end of the Old Mori Trail at 0.5 mile, turn right to continue on the flat promenade parallel to the ocean and Sharp Park Beach. This is also the California Coastal Trail. Note: You'll avoid the stairs and the steep Mori Peak Trail, but you'll also miss Mori Point. Turn around whenever you like and return the way you came.

For a more moderate option that avoids the steep ascent up Mori Peak and cuts 0.2 mile off the route, follow the directions up to Mori Point and back to the top of the Bootlegger's Steps. From there, take the Coastal Trail toward the Lishumsha Trail, then follow the route as described above.

3 Sweeney Ridge

DISTANCE: 6 miles
ELEVATION GAIN: 960 feet
HIGH POINT: 1,220 feet
DIFFICULTY: Moderate
TIME: 2 hours and 15 minutes
FITNESS: Hikers, fit walkers, runners
FAMILY-FRIENDLY: This route is best for families with older children due to the elevation gain.
DOG-FRIENDLY: Yes, on leash
AMENITIES: Restroom, benches
CONTACT: Golden Gate National Recreation Area
BEFORE YOU GO: The first 1.7 miles of the route are paved, so it's even terrain on this stretch.
GPS: 37° 37' 9.9048" N, 122° 27' 15.0804" W

GETTING THERE

Map to: Sneath Lane Trail Parking, Sneath Lane, San Bruno. **Public Transit:** SamTrans bus 141 stops at Sneath Lane and Mendocino Court, a 0.7-mile walk to the hike start. **Parking:** There is a free parking area at the start of the hike, but it can fill up quickly on weekends.

This route is as steeped in history as it is in fog. In 1769, Spain sent Captain Juan Gaspar de Portolá, sixty-four men, and two hundred horses and mules from San Diego on an overland route to look for Monterey Bay. Unable to find it, Portolá continued north to present-day Pacifica.

Once there, the Aramai, a local Ohlone tribelet, accompanied the explorers to Sweeney Ridge, where they were the first Europeans to see the San Francisco Bay. The Spanish "discovery" of the Bay was sadly the beginning of the end of the Ohlone way of life. Seven years later, the Anza Expedition left New Spain (Mexico) to head north and colonize the area and its people.

Come here to contemplate history and hike this 1,220-foot-high ridgeline that has been part of the Golden Gate National Recreation Area since 1987. And in case you're wondering, no one knows for sure why it's called Sweeney Ridge. It's an unsolved Pacifica mystery . . .

GET MOVING

Pick up the Sneath Lane Trail and continue for 1.7 miles. The paved trail heads gently downhill and is lined by flora like coyote brush, poison oak, yarrow, mustard, fennel, and blackberry. Soon the trail starts heading uphill. You'll see coastal sage, eucalyptus, and toyon.

At 0.5 mile, take in your first views of the Bay. San Andreas Lake is ahead and to the left. You can see San Francisco International Airport's air traffic control tower and runways as well as Coyote Point. At 0.9 mile, the South San Francisco

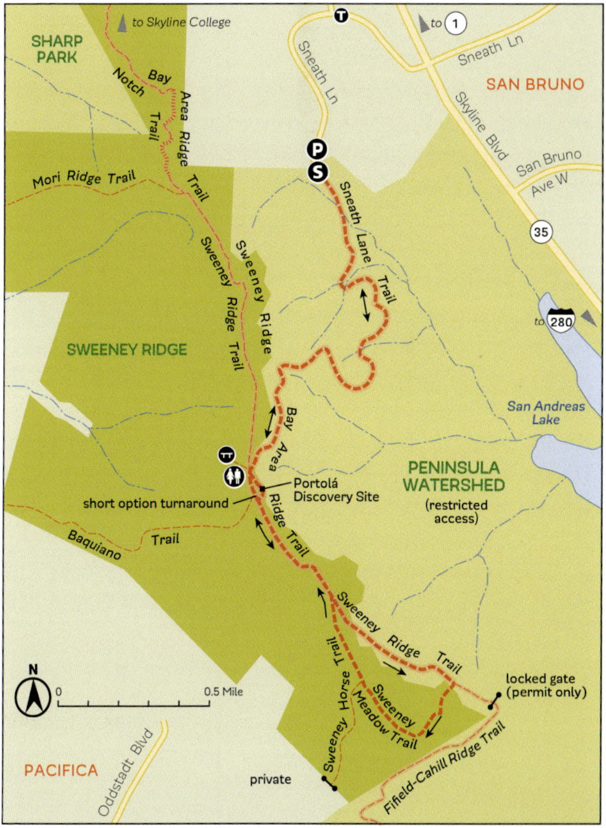

Industrial City sign appears behind you. Just after this, "FOG LINE" is painted onto the trail.

At 1.5 miles, you'll enter a grove of eucalyptus and toyon, and at 1.7 miles you'll reach the restroom and a bench looking out at the ocean or the fog, depending on the weather. To visit the Portolá Discovery Site, turnaround left at the restroom to pick up the Sweeney Ridge Trail (part of the Bay Area Ridge Trail). The trail flattens out and is now dirt. Within a few hundred feet, look for a trail on your left that takes you to the site. (If you've reached the Baquiano Trail that turns off to the right, you've gone about 50 feet too far.)

There are two monuments at this site on Sweeney Ridge: one commemorating the Portolá expedition and another commemorating Carl Patrick McCarthy, who brought 11,863 visitors to this site between 1966 and 1981. As of this writing, the monument for Portolá's "discovery" has been boarded up. Through a contemporary lens, it seems unreasonable to call this a "discovery" site when the Aramai people were living here for generations. You can read more about the Portolá expedition and the reinterpretation of the "discovery" site next to the monuments.

This spot is a great turnaround point for a 3.6-mile hike with 660 feet of total elevation gain. If you like, head back to the start the way you came. To continue on the 6-mile route, stay on the Sweeney Ridge Trail. You're surrounded on both sides by scrub plants. After half a mile, stay straight on the Sweeney Ridge Trail as the Sweeney Horse Trail heads off to the right.

At 2.8 miles, turn right on the Sweeney Meadow Trail toward the Sweeney Horse Trail. Then, in half a mile, follow

From the high ridgeline, you can see all the way to the Bay on a clear day.

the Sweeney Horse Trail toward the Sweeney Ridge Trail. This section of trail is narrower than the other trails on this route. When you arrive at the Sweeney Ridge Trail, turn left and return the way you came all the way back to the start.

GO FARTHER

Hike Sweeney Ridge from another starting point, such as Shelldance Gardens (dog-friendly) or Skyline College (no dogs allowed).

4 Pedro Point Headlands and Devil's Slide

DISTANCE: 5.5 miles
ELEVATION GAIN: 1,120 feet
HIGH POINT: 650 feet
DIFFICULTY: Challenging
TIME: 1 hour and 40 minutes
FITNESS: Hikers, runners. Walkers can see Make It Shorter.
FAMILY-FRIENDLY: Families can see Make It Shorter.
DOG-FRIENDLY: Yes, on leash
AMENITIES: Restrooms, benches, bike repair station, overlooks on the Devil's Slide Trail
CONTACT: Pacifica Land Trust and County of San Mateo
BEFORE YOU GO: You may want to bring hiking poles for the Pedro Point Headlands section of the route. Devil's Slide is accessible, but steep in sections.
GPS: 37° 35' 6.9684" N, 122° 30' 34.92" W

GETTING THERE

Map to: Devil's Slide Trail north parking lot, Pacifica. **Public Transit:** Take SamTrans bus 117 to the Devil's Slide Tunnel stop. This stop leaves you near the Devil's Slide south parking lot. **Parking:** The Devil's Slide Trail north entrance has two small, free parking lots. Spots fill up quickly.

This two-in-one route is an easy way to explore two vastly different areas of Pacifica while taking in stunning ocean views. The Pedro Point Headlands feature rugged dirt trails with some steep inclines and descents. In 2.6 miles, you'll see most of the trails here and enjoy views from 600 feet above the Pacific.

Egg Rock, a.k.a Devil's Slide Rock, is visible from the Bluff Trail. (Photo: Yasaman Mohsenin)

Devil's Slide is a paved multiuse trail 200 feet above the ocean on a former segment of Highway 1. Here you'll stay on a single paved road the whole time and then return to the start. The name "Devil's Slide" comes from the cliffs here, which are prone to rockslides. This section of Highway 1 was troubled from its opening in 1937, often closing periodically due to landslides, which caused long detours. After a brutal storm in 1995 closed the road for five months, San Mateo County voters decided to reroute the highway on a new road with tunnels passing through San Pedro Mountain. These tunnels were completed in 2013 and at 4,200 feet long they are the longest in the state. The Devil's Slide Trail is now a part of the California Coastal Trail.

If you're not up for 5.5 miles, you can tackle half of the route instead. Both hikes start and end in the same place, so choose your own adventure!

GET MOVING

To hike the trail to Pedro Point, take a sidewalk on the north side of Highway 1 and continue onto a wide asphalt path. Soon, you pick up a dirt trail uphill until you arrive at informational signage in a clearing. Here, turn right following a sign for the Arroyo Trail and Pacifica. When the trail almost immediately splits, stay left to quickly enter the woods. Turn right on the unmarked Middle Ridge Trail at 0.6 mile, passing a turn on the right toward Pacifica partway through this stretch. Over the next 0.3 mile, you'll climb 200 feet through wooded and then exposed areas. Two-thirds of the way through this stretch, you may see a hand-crafted stone labyrinth along the trail.

At 0.9 mile, stay straight to pick up the Bluff Trail. Don't turn left here or take the social trail to the right. Follow the Bluff Trail 0.3 mile to its end, passing the North Ridge Trail on your right halfway through this stretch. The ocean is on your left, Shelter Cove Beach is on your right, and San Pedro Rock is ahead of you. At the end of the trail at 1.2 miles, enjoy views of Mount Tamalpais, San Francisco, and Pacifica.

Turn around and take the Bluff Trail 0.4 mile, bearing right at the Middle Ridge Trail junction where you were before. At 1.6 miles, stay straight to pick up the South Ridge Trail at a junction with the Arroyo Trail.

Take this trail for 0.6 mile. After an initial ascent, you descend the rest of the way, passing pine trees and seeing (from east to west) Montara Mountain's North Peak, Peak Mountain, and San Pedro Mountain in the distance. At the junction with informational signage, turn right to head back to the parking area.

To take the Devil's Slide Trail, start at the far end of the larger parking lot. From here, follow the paved trail uphill for 0.3 mile and then downhill for 1 mile. When you reach the restroom and other parking area, turn around and return the way you came.

As you hike, look for former US Army bunkers perched on the hillside. Also, keep an eye out for local birds. This area is home to sooty shearwaters, common murres, pelicans, and many other species.

MAKE IT SHORTER

Do just half of the route at a time! The Pedro Point Headlands half of the hike is 2.6 miles with 670 feet of elevation gain, and the Devil's Slide half of the route is 2.6 miles with 350 feet of elevation gain.

5 Pillar Point Bluff and Mavericks Beach

DISTANCE: 3.3 miles
ELEVATION GAIN: 210 feet
HIGH POINT: 190 feet
DIFFICULTY: Easy
TIME: 1 hour and 45 minutes
FITNESS: Hikers, walkers, runners
FAMILY-FRIENDLY: Yes
DOG-FRIENDLY: Yes, on leash
AMENITIES: Restrooms, benches, accessible trails (Jean Lauer Trail)
CONTACT: County of San Mateo (Pillar Point Bluff), City of Half Moon Bay (Mavericks Beach)
GPS: 37° 30' 6.5844" N, 122° 29' 48.39" W

GETTING THERE

Map to: Enter West Point parking lot into your mapping app and continue to the end of West Point Avenue to locate the lot closest to the start of the hike. **Public Transit:** SamTrans bus 117 stops at Airport Street and Harvard Avenue, a 0.5-mile walk to the start. Note: There are no sidewalks. **Parking:** Free parking. The lot at the end of West Point Avenue has more than forty spaces but fills up quickly. If the lot is full, you can wait for a spot or park 0.3 mile away at the West Point parking lot.

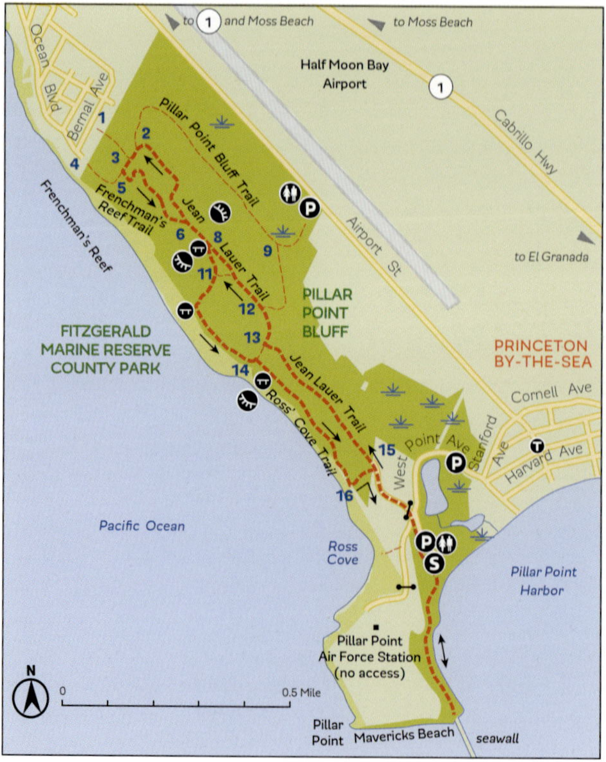

Cheerful wildflowers line the Ross' Cove Trail.

Half Moon Bay transports you a world away from city life. Feel your cares melt away as you stroll above the Pacific and breathe in the ocean air. On the selected route, you'll hike a loop around Pillar Point Bluff, then head to Mavericks Beach. Aside from one short ascent/descent, the trails are flat, making this a great area for most hikers to explore.

On this route, there's no missing the golf ball–shaped dome at Pillar Point Air Force Station. This is a protective shell for a telemetry antenna that tracks satellites and missiles fired from Vandenberg Space Force Base, 275 miles south of here. You'll also enjoy Mavericks Beach, which has hosted big wave surfing competitions since 1998. Mavericks Beach was named for a local surfer's dog. It's also synonymous with local surfer Jeff Clark, who rode these waves for fifteen years before the larger surfing community discovered them.

GET MOVING

From the parking lot entrance, look for a door-shaped section of a yellow gate to pick up the Jean Lauer Trail, named for a Peninsula Open Space Trust (POST) employee who dedicated herself to the coastside. POST purchased and restored the land before the San Mateo County Parks Department acquired it in 2011. The trail starts out paved and quickly turns to dirt. You'll be on this trail for 1.2 miles. Along the way, you will encounter several trail junctions that you will also see on the map. However, I only note here those that you need to pay attention to.

As you head uphill, some pine trees and a variety of smaller flora (including yarrow, coyote brush, blackberry, poison oak, and fennel) may line the trail, depending on the season. After 0.3 mile, reach a T at a marker for trail junction 13. Stay right.

At 0.6 mile, stay right at junction 6 to stay on the Jean Lauer Trail. The mountains you see on your right belong to Rancho Corral de Tierra. At 1 mile, you will start to see homes in front of you as the trail arcs left toward the ocean. Shortly after this, turn left at the second of two junction 3 markers to pick up the Frenchman's Reef Trail. This trail parallels the Jean Lauer Trail but is closer to the ocean.

At 1.4 miles at junction 6, merge onto the Jean Lauer Trail. Then, 300 feet later, take a right at junction 8 to pick up the

Ross' Cove Trail. After a 400 feet, stay right at junction 11. On this 1-mile stretch of trail you'll get closer-up views of the ocean and the Air Force station. You may see mustard, sticky monkey flower, and the occasional cypress along the trail.

At 1.8 miles, check out the expansive ocean views at an overlook. Walk by a bench to stay on the trail. Then after 0.3 mile, make a left at junction 16 to head back to the paved portion of the Jean Lauer Trail. The trail splits partway through this stretch; stay right.

To continue to Mavericks Beach, head back to the parking lot and walk to the far side of it to pick up a wide gravel trail behind the "West Shoreline Access" sign. Stay straight on this gravel trail for about 0.2 mile until it drops you on the beach. Here you can continue on the beach or a trail slightly above the beach. Keep going another 0.3 mile until you reach a seawall and a warning about the waves. Return the way you came.

GO FARTHER

Head north to the Moss Beach section of the Fitzgerald Marine Reserve. Here you can stroll through the dramatic Seal Cove Cypress Tree Tunnels and visit the tide pools (check the tide tables before visiting).

Next page: Edgewood Park (Hike 8) showcases broad Bay views a short jaunt from several Peninsula cities.

MIDPENINSULA

Mention of the San Francisco Peninsula can conjure up images of the 101 and 280 highways, densely populated cities, and tech companies. This chapter aims to show you a different side of the Peninsula—one rich with redwoods, oak woodlands, grasslands, and wildlife. Most of the hikes in this chapter are just minutes from major Peninsula cities and towns. While you may hear some highway noise on these trails from time to time, the nature that's within reach just a quick jaunt away from civilization is more than worth it.

This section starts on the Sawyer Camp Trail, part of the larger Crystal Springs Regional Trail. Here you'll stroll along flat, accessible trails alongside the Lower Crystal Springs Reservoir. To the west of this reservoir and perched high atop a ridge is the Fifield-Cahill Ridge Trail that lets you experience a protected area of the San Francisco Bay Watershed. South of here, Edgewood County Park and Natural Reserve is a playground for hikers, trail runners, and horseback riders alike. Enjoy scenic views and visit the education center to learn about this park's rare flora and fauna. Just across the street from here is Pulgas Ridge Open Space Preserve, a pup-lover's paradise with oak-lined trails, ridgeline views, and a sizable off-leash area. To close out this chapter, you'll explore two trails in Woodside. Huddart Park boasts trails shaded by second-growth redwoods and the Peninsula AIDS Memorial Grove, and Wunderlich County Park brings you into horse country. This park has redwoods, horse-friendly trails, and a historic district that includes a stable, carriage house, and more—all formerly owned by the Folger family of coffee fame.

6 Sawyer Camp Trail

DISTANCE:	Up to 7 miles
ELEVATION GAIN:	50 feet
HIGH POINT:	330 feet
DIFFICULTY:	Easy
TIME:	2 to 3 hours for a 6- to 7-mile walk
FITNESS:	Hikers, walkers, runners
FAMILY-FRIENDLY:	Yes
DOG-FRIENDLY:	No
AMENITIES:	Restrooms, benches, picnic tables, accessible trail
CONTACT:	County of San Mateo
GPS:	37° 31' 51.3156" N, 122° 21' 50.544" W

GETTING THERE

Map to: Sawyer Camp Trail South Trailhead 950 CA-35, Redwood City. **Parking:** Free street parking is available on Skyline Boulevard.

While you don't really need directions for the Sawyer Camp Trail, I wanted to include this route because according to the San Mateo County Parks website, this is the best-known and most-used trail in the entire county park system.

This is one of three segments of the planned 17.5-mile Crystal Springs Regional Trail (the other segments are the San Andreas and Crystal Springs segments). When complete, the route will extend from San Bruno to Woodside. The trail is paved, flat, accessible, and multiuse, making it perfect for walkers, runners, bikers, wheelchair users, and families pushing strollers. It's peaceful, and I've never visited without seeing deer.

The trail name refers to Leander Sawyer, who bought this land in 1853. The route you'll hike here was Sawyer's path to his camp, where he ran an inn providing food and shelter to travelers passing through the area. This route became a stagecoach road and later a car road until 1978.

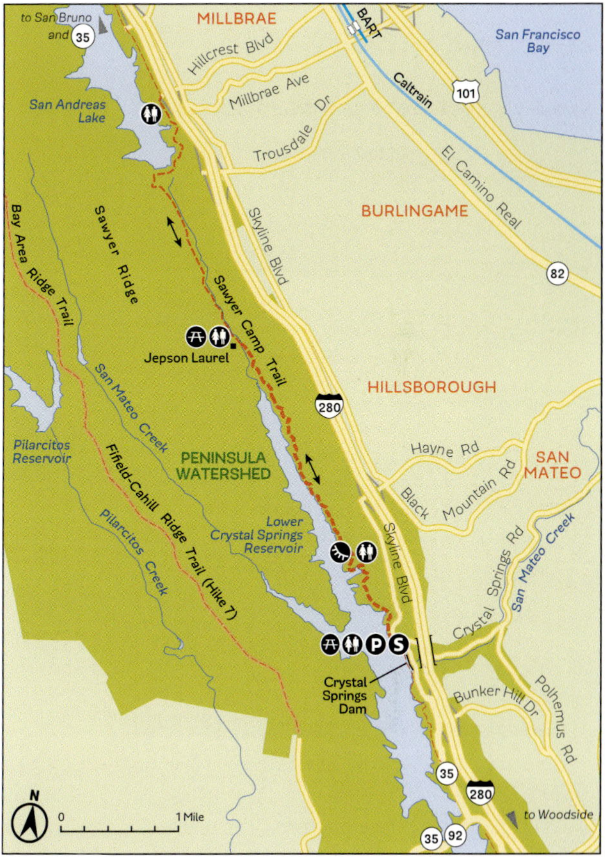

GET MOVING

Start your hike at the Sawyer Camp Trail South Trailhead at the intersection of Skyline Boulevard and Crystal Springs Road. Walk through the gate and past the restrooms. Just beyond the restrooms, there is a turnoff to your left.

Stay straight here (or take the left to take a 0.2-mile roundtrip visit to the Crystal Springs Dam; see Go Farther). As

Sunlight shines through the trees on the Sawyer Camp Trail.

you hike, you'll soon begin to pass the lovely Crystal Springs Reservoir. You'll see mile markers every half a mile to help you keep track of your distance if you don't have a device to track your hike. If you continue past the 3-mile marker, you'll soon reach the northern end of the Lower (northern) Crystal Springs Reservoir.

Just before you reach the 3.5-mile marker, you'll see a restroom and the Jepson Laurel area, which commemorates a 600-year-old bay laurel tree that's the oldest and largest of its kind in California. In 1923, it was named for Willis Linn Jepson, the creator of *The Jepson Manual*, a guide for identifying California plant species. The tree is behind a fence, and its location is marked with a small monument. The monument says the tree is the "second-largest laurel in California," as it was at the time of the monument's dedication. However, the former largest laurel that grew along the Russian River near Cloverdale has since been chopped down for covering too much hayfield.

Once you've finished taking in the beauty of this centuries-old tree, turn around and retrace your steps to return to the Sawyer Camp Trail South Trailhead.

GO FARTHER

Visit the Crystal Springs Dam. Built in 1888, it created the Lower (northern) Crystal Springs Reservoir. There are two other reservoirs created by other dams that are part of the Crystal Springs Regional Trail: the Upper (southern) Crystal Springs Reservoir, just south of the Lower Reservoir and this dam, and the San Andreas Lake at the northern end of the Sawyer Camp Trail.

While some of the water in these reservoirs comes from local creeks or rainfall, most is pumped in from Yosemite National Park's Hetch Hetchy Reservoir. The water you see here provides drinking water for San Francisco and also serves as a backup and emergency water source for the area. On an interesting geological note, the San Andreas Fault lies about 1,100 feet east of the dam and runs along the Sawyer Camp Trail! Don't worry, the dam has survived both the 1906 and 1989 earthquakes with minimal damage.

If you return to this area on your bike, you can also visit the Pulgas Water Temple, a monument commemorating the completion of the Hetch Hetchy water system. Note: Car parking is limited and only available on weekdays.

7 Fifield-Cahill Ridge Trail

DISTANCE: Up to 10 miles, depending on the docent-led tour
ELEVATION GAIN: 920 to 1,920 feet
HIGH POINT: 1,160 feet
DIFFICULTY: Moderate to difficult
TIME: Depends on distance and group pace
FITNESS: Hikers, walkers
FAMILY-FRIENDLY: This route is best for families with older children due to the elevation gain and docent-led tour. Younger children can hike the publicly-accessible, barrier-free Watershed Discovery Loop.
DOG-FRIENDLY: No
AMENITIES: Restrooms every 2 miles along the trail
CONTACT: San Francisco Public Utilities Commission (SFPUC)
BEFORE YOU GO: No public access. A free permit is required for this docent-led tour. Book your hike on the trail's page of the SFPUC website (www.sfpuc.gov). Bring your own food and water; no water is available on the trail. Accessible hikes are available upon request.
GPS: 37° 29' 46.7988" N, 122° 22' 0.5052" W

GETTING THERE

Map to: Skylawn Funeral Home, Memorial Park, and Crematory, San Mateo. **Public Transit:** SamTrans bus 294 stops at the intersection of Skyline Boulevard and CA-92. You will then need a ride through the cemetery to the trailhead. **Parking:** When you sign up for an event, you will receive parking instructions from someone at the SFPUC a few days before the hike.

The Fifield-Cahill Ridge Trail is a unique opportunity to explore a permit-only section of the Bay Area Ridge Trail. The trail is part of the San Francisco Watershed, which is operated by the SFPUC. The watershed comprises 23,000 acres and contains the Crystal Springs, Pilarcitos, and San Andreas

Reservoirs, which provide drinking water to 2.8 million people in four Bay Area counties.

The 10-mile trail is marked in one-mile increments and extends between Skyline Quarry in San Mateo and Sweeney Ridge in Pacifica. It traverses a variety of habitats, including

Colorful spring widflowers seen along the Fifield-Cahill Ridge Trail. (Photo: Candice Byrum)

coniferous forests, oak woodlands, and serpentine grasslands. A state-designated fish and game refuge, it contains the highest concentration of rare, threatened, and endangered flora and fauna in the Bay Area. The trail's name comes from two previous landowners: W. J. Fifield, who operated a 1,000-acre dairy farm along Pilarcitos Creek, and the Cahill family, who owned and farmed 400 acres along Pilarcitos Creek and what's now known as Cahill Ridge.

To learn more about the trail and to reserve spots for a hike, visit the trail's page of the SFPUC website. If available and fitness permitting, I recommend choosing a hike that's at least 11 miles long roundtrip so you can reach the best views on this trail.

GET MOVING

Most hikes start at the cemetery gate on the former Cahill family lands. From here, a wide gravel service road leads you through a thick forest of oaks, bay laurels, and Douglas-firs. At times, you'll get views of the Pilarcitos Creek Watershed to the west. After about 4 miles, you reach Five Points, a major intersection. Many hiking routes turn around here.

If you venture beyond Five Points, the trees quickly thin out, and you'll walk through grasslands and coastal scrub. Between mile markers 5 and 6, you'll enter into the former Fifield farmland and get views of Pilarcitos Reservoir. At mile marker 8, you'll take in views of Pacifica and the ocean. And between mile markers 6 and 10, you'll enjoy views of the Bay, the Peninsula, San Bruno Mountain, Mount Diablo, and San Francisco. The Portola Gate marks the end of this trail where you will enjoy stunning 360-degree views. If you've made it this far, you'll hike 8.5 miles back to the start at the cemetery gate.

GO FARTHER

Hikers can visit Skylawn Memorial Park (part of the Bay Area Ridge Trail) during regular business hours. Docent-led tours are not required as long as you stay on the cemetery property.

BAY AREA RIDGE TRAIL

When it is complete, the Bay Area Ridge Trail will encircle the entire San Francisco Bay Area with 550 miles of continuous trail. Since 1989, more than 375 miles have been knit together to complete the vision to build a hiking, cycling, and equestrian trail on the ridgelines around the Bay Area. Existing parks and open space have been connected, and gaps are actively being addressed by land management agencies and nonprofit groups to acquire land and build trail to fulfill this ambitious vision. Eighteen routes in this book run along parts of the Bay Area Ridge Trail, and you will come across references to it in the text and on the maps. To learn more about the Bay Area Ridge Trail, visit ridgetrail.org.

8 Edgewood Park and Natural Preserve

DISTANCE: 3.5 miles
ELEVATION GAIN: 650 feet
HIGH POINT: 800 feet
DIFFICULTY: Moderate
TIME: 1 hour and 45 minutes
FITNESS: Hikers, walkers, runners
FAMILY-FRIENDLY: Yes, families will enjoy a visit to the Bill and Jean Lane Education Center.
DOG-FRIENDLY: No
AMENITIES: Restrooms, benches, picnic area, education center. Check the "Edgewood Park & Natural Preserve" page on the County of San Mateo website for center hours.
CONTACT: County of San Mateo
GPS: 37° 28' 23.5848" N, 122° 16' 41.736" W

GETTING THERE

Map to: 10 Old Stage Coach Road, Redwood City. **Parking:** Free parking. This preserve has two lots: one off Edgewood Road and the other on Old Stage Coach Road. You can hike this route from either one.

Edgewood County Park and Natural Preserve is nature made accessible. Located just off Interstate 280 and a ten-minute drive from San Carlos, it's a local favorite for hikers, trail runners, and equestrians. On this route, you'll climb through chaparral, oak woodland, and grassland habitats to reach a viewpoint looking out toward the Peninsula, Bay, and Mount Diablo. For me, the highlight of the hike comes toward the end of the route when you descend on winding trails just after the viewpoint to even better Peninsula and Bay views.

Before or after the hike, head to the Bill and Jean Lane Education Center to learn more about the flora that thrives in this park's serpentine soil; the native fauna that live here, including the endangered Bay checkerspot butterfly; and the human history behind the park—all in an environmentally friendly building. Between 1959 and 1990, Bill Lane was the publisher of *Sunset* magazine, which celebrates travel, home design, gardening, and recipes of the American West.

GET MOVING

Start the hike at the Bill and Jean Lane Education Center. Head up the stairs that start on the side of the building and then go behind it. At the top of the stairway, turn right to pick up the Edgewood Trail. Surrounding you are scrub

Edgewood Park and Natural Preserve is 467 acres of nature just a ten-minute drive from downtown San Carlos.

plants and oaks, toyons, and bay laurels, as well as plentiful poison oak (watch out!).

Stay on the Edgewood Trail for 1.2 miles, passing markers 4 and 5 about half a mile into this stretch and marker 9 toward the end of it. During this first climb, you'll gain around 370 feet. Continue on the Edgewood Trail to marker 13 at 1.3 miles. Here you're as close as you'll get to Interstate 280.

At marker 13, turn left on the Ridgeview Trail. Stay on this trail for 0.6 mile, passing marker 15 and then continuing on to marker 17. Along this stretch, the highway noise decreases. At marker 17, head right and uphill 425 feet to reach a viewpoint. Here you can take in panoramic views of the Peninsula, the Bay, and Mount Diablo from a well-placed bench. You are now at the highest elevation on this hike: just over 800 feet. When you're done at the viewpoint, head back to marker 17 at 2.1 miles.

This time, at marker 17, turn right and head downhill on the Live Oak Trail. At 2.2 miles, reach marker 19, turn left, and head downhill on the Serpentine Trail. You can see sweeping views of the Peninsula and Mount Diablo from here—I like these unobstructed views even better than those at the viewpoint with the bench. Here you'll also see the switchbacks that will take you down to marker 16 at 2.4 miles.

At marker 16, bear right to pick up the Sylvan Trail. After half a mile, continue on the Sylvan Trail toward the 2.0-mile marker for the Sylvan Trail Exercise Loop. You'll be on this trail another 0.4 mile to reach marker 7 at 3.3 miles.

At marker 7, bear right and continue downhill. In 0.1 mile, reach marker 3, where you head over a bridge and continue 250 feet farther to end the hike in the Edgewood Road parking lot or back at the education center.

GO FARTHER

Check out dog-friendly Pulgas Ridge Open Space Preserve (Hike 9) just 0.4 mile away on the other side of Edgewood Road.

9 Pulgas Ridge Open Space Preserve

DISTANCE: 4.1 miles
ELEVATION GAIN: 720 feet
HIGH POINT: 810 feet
DIFFICULTY: Moderate
TIME: 2 hours
FITNESS: Hikers, fit walkers, runners
FAMILY-FRIENDLY: Families can take the flat and accessible Cordilleras Trail for a shorter, easier hike.
DOG-FRIENDLY: Yes, on leash for all trails, plus one off-leash section off the Hassler Trail (just off this route)
AMENITIES: Restrooms, benches, accessible trails
CONTACT: Midpeninsula Regional Open Space District
BEFORE YOU GO: The preserve is right off Interstate 280, so while it's convenient to get to, you may hear highway noise on the trails.
GPS: 37° 28' 29.7408" N, 122° 16' 59.0592" W

GETTING THERE

Map to: Pulgas Ridge parking lot, 167 Edmonds Road, Redwood City. **Public Transit:** Take SamTrans bus 61 to the Brittan Avenue and Crestview Drive stop. From there, you're 0.2 mile from the start. Use caution, as there aren't sidewalks the whole way. **Parking:** Free parking. The parking lot has twenty-three standard spaces and two ADA spaces.

This route helps you cover four of Pulgas Ridge Open Space Preserve's 6 miles of trails. You'll hike two short, accessible trails, then continue to narrow singletrack trails, meandering through oak woodlands, exploring a ridgeline with soaring views, and descending back to your starting point. You'll see ample oaks, bay laurels, toyons, and manzanitas, plus scrub plants like broom and California sagebrush.

This 366-acre preserve is a dream for dogs. All the trails here are dog-friendly, and there's even a 17.5-acre off-leash area off the Hassler Loop Trail (just off the selected route)—a rarity for Peninsula parks. There's also some interesting history here: Pulgas Ridge was once the site of the Hassler Health Home, a tuberculosis sanitarium owned by the City of San Francisco that operated between 1927 and 1972. In 1983, the Midpeninsula Regional Open Space District bought this land, and the sanitarium was demolished in 1985.

GET MOVING

Start the route at the eastern end of the parking lot (near the lot entrance). Pick up the Cordilleras Connector Trail, a flat gravel trail resembling a sidewalk. After 0.1 mile, turn left when you come to a T with a wide, flat, paved trail lined by a grassy area. Stay on the Cordilleras Trail for 0.3 mile. You're almost at the end of this stretch when you reach a small peach-colored building. Here, bear right off the paved trail to pick up a dirt trail along a wood fence.

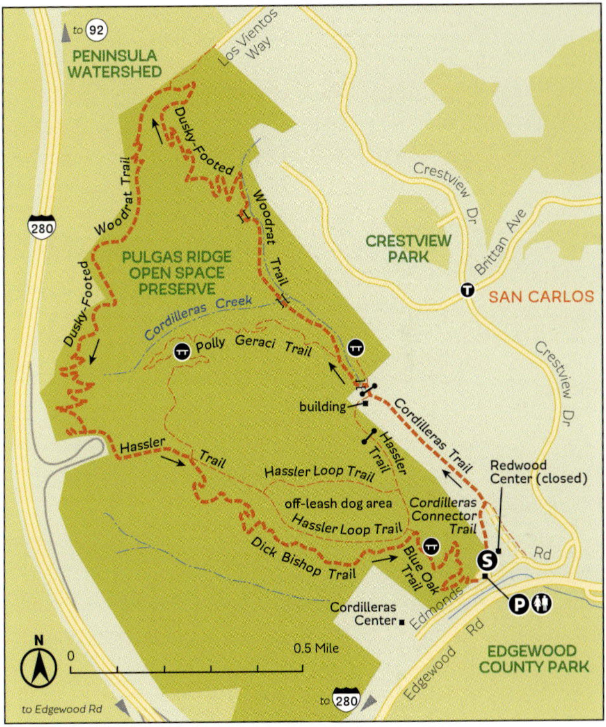

Follow this dirt trail a short distance, then turn left and cross a bridge toward the Polly Geraci and Dusky-Footed Woodrat Trails. The singletrack Polly Geraci Trail is dedicated to Anna Pauline (Polly) Geraci, a local hiker and conservationist. It was named for Geraci after she died in a car accident in 1988. After 0.1 mile on this trail (0.6 mile total), bear right to pick up the singletrack Dusky-Footed Woodrat Trail, named for the small rodents who live in these woodlands. You'll be on this trail for 2.2 miles, until 2.8 miles total.

For the first half of the Dusky-Footed Woodrat Trail (1.1 miles), you'll hike partially shaded trails through woodlands

The first half of the Dusky-Footed Woodrat Trail is shaded by oaks, bay laurels, and toyon.

with coast live oaks, bay laurels, and toyons. This section starts out flat and then takes several switchbacks to climb to this route's highest elevation—810 feet. By the end of this stretch, you'll be on exposed trails.

For the second half of this trail (1.1 miles), you'll alternate between descending and hiking along a ridge, enjoying views of surrounding homes and the Santa Cruz Mountains. The flora around you changes too. You'll see manzanita, coastal scrub, California sagebrush, and broom. You might hear airplanes and traffic from Interstate 280. The end of this section features several switchbacks that bring you closer to the highway.

After the full 2.2 miles on this trail (2.8 miles total), you drop onto the Hassler Trail, a wide paved and gravel trail. Here you can head right for a quick detour to an overlook that is underwhelming looking west but gives you views of the Bay to the east. Head downhill for 0.2 mile and bear right to pick up the singletrack dirt Dick Bishop Trail. On a clear day, you can see Mount Hamilton's Lick Observatory to the southeast. (If you have a dog with you, you can also stay on the Hassler Trail to enter the off-leash dog area.)

Stay on the Dick Bishop Trail for 0.7 mile, winding through areas with views and then descending back into the trees. When you reach the Blue Oak Trail, turn right and head downhill on gradual switchbacks to reach the parking lot where you started.

GO FARTHER

Explore the off-leash dog area of the Hassler Trail.

10 Huddart Park

DISTANCE:	4.7 miles
ELEVATION GAIN:	930 feet
HIGH POINT:	1,490 feet
DIFFICULTY:	Moderate
TIME:	2 hours
FITNESS:	Hikers, runners
FAMILY-FRIENDLY:	Families can do a shorter hike. There's also a playground near the Werder picnic area.
DOG-FRIENDLY:	No
AMENITIES:	Restrooms, benches, water, picnic areas, playground
CONTACT:	County of San Mateo
GPS:	37° 26' 29.6988" N, 122° 17' 27.1212" W

GETTING THERE

Map to: Huddart Park, 1100 Kings Mountain Road, Woodside.
Parking: Park in the Zwierlein picnic area. Pay a small fee to park at the park entrance (cash only).

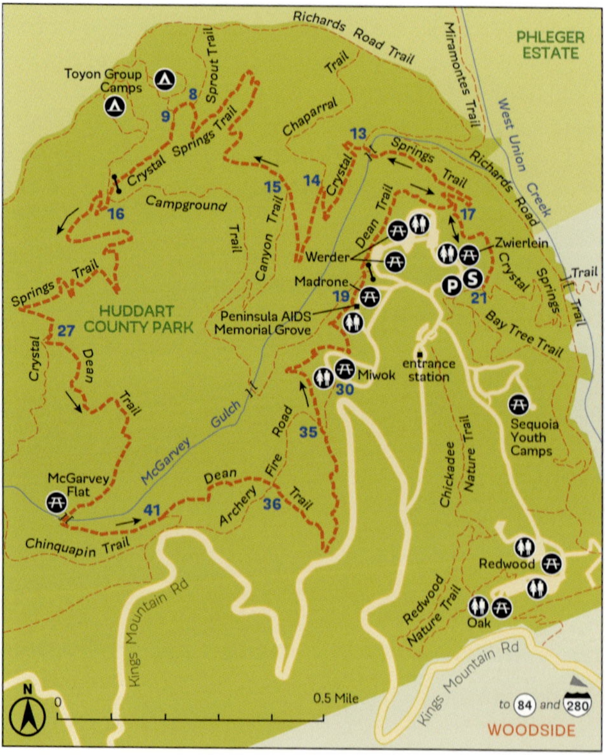

Huddart Park makes redwoods accessible. You won't find towering thousand-year-old trees here, but second-growth redwoods are plentiful. And you'll get to experience them without the Muir Woods crowds, just twenty minutes from Redwood City and thirty minutes from San Jose.

Getting around the selected route is simple. You'll spend just over half the route ascending the Crystal Springs Trail and just under half the route descending the Dean Trail. The trails here are serene anytime, but during the rainy season, you'll enjoy seasonal waterfalls, and in warmer months, the tree cover that shades virtually the entire route is a saving grace.

Second-growth redwoods line the trails in Huddart Park.

There's a small, yet poignant stop at the end of this route: the Peninsula AIDS Memorial Grove. Look for a ring of redwoods next to the Miwok parking area. The brainchild of a community group, the grove was dedicated on October 5, 1997, to people whose lives were affected by the AIDS epidemic.

GET MOVING

From the Zwierlein Picnic Area parking lot, look for trail marker 21, and head left to pick up the Crystal Springs Trail.

You'll be on this trail for 2.5 miles until you reach the Dean Trail at marker 27. The fully shaded route is lined with redwoods, Douglas-firs, oaks, and bay laurels. Watch out for poison oak.

Follow the Crystal Springs Trail through a series of junctions as you gain 850 feet: At marker 17, stay straight; at marker 13, turn left and cross two bridges; at marker 14, go left; and at marker 15 at 1 mile, keep straight. Continue a little over half a mile farther to marker 8, where you bear left, then left again 500 feet later at marker 9. In just under 0.2 mile, you reach marker 16, where the Crystal Springs Trail heads straight through a gate crossing the wide Campground Trail. From here it's 0.7 mile to marker 27 and the Dean Trail (2.5 miles total). A quarter mile through this stretch, you'll reach the only view on this route—the Bay, Peninsula, and mountains in the distance alongside some electrical towers.

At marker 27, where the Crystal Springs Trail branches off to the right, stay straight to pick up the Dean Trail—where you will stay for the remaining 2.2 miles back to the start.

In just under a half mile, reach McGarvey Flat, an area with a bench and picnic table that looks over McGarvey Gulch, a peaceful creek. This is a pleasant place to rest for a snack or lunch while you listen to the water flowing by. At marker 41 (3.2 miles), stay left and head downhill, then cross the Archery Fire Road at marker 36. At marker 35, take a quick jog left and then right to cross Archery Fire Road again, staying on the narrower Dean Trail. Continue another 0.2 mile to marker 30 and the Miwok picnic area.

Pass this picnic area and continue another 0.2 mile to the Madrone picnic area. At the parking lot by the restroom, take a quick detour off the trail to visit the Peninsula AIDS Memorial Grove, a ring of redwoods (there is a small sign at the base of the trees). Return to the trail where you left it, and in a few hundred feet reach marker 19. Cross the Campground Trail and walk 0.2 mile to junction 17, your original intersection with the Crystal Springs Trail. Turn right and walk the final 0.2 mile back to the parking lot.

GO FARTHER

Savor your time near the redwoods by having a picnic at one of the park's many picnic areas.

11 Wunderlich County Park

DISTANCE:	4.9 miles
ELEVATION GAIN:	960 feet
HIGH POINT:	1,460 feet
DIFFICULTY:	Moderate
TIME:	2 hours and 30 minutes
FITNESS:	Hikers, runners
FAMILY-FRIENDLY:	Families can hike to Salamander Flat or visit the Folger Estate and Carriage Room Museum.
DOG-FRIENDLY:	No
AMENITIES:	Restrooms, benches, water, horseback riding, bike parking, historic sites, museum
CONTACT:	County of San Mateo
GPS:	37° 24' 38.9448" N, 122° 15' 40.5864" W

GETTING THERE

Map to: Lower Wunderlich parking, 4040 Woodside Road, Woodside. **Parking:** Free parking is available in the large Lower Wunderlich parking lot.

Wunderlich County Park transports you right into horse country. There are tie racks in the parking lot, horse-friendly trails, and trail rides. There's also the Folger (of the coffee fame) Estate Stable Historic Distric, which includes a main stable and carriage house (now the Carriage Room Museum) that date back to 1905–1906. Arthur Brown, Jr., in partnership

Wunderlich is an escape to horse country that enchants people of all ages.

with Henry Schulze, designed these buildings. Brown later became famous for his work on San Francisco's Coit Tower and War Memorial Opera House and Stanford's Hoover Tower. On a short self-guided tour, you can also check out an 1874 "dairy house" (a structure used to preserve food before refrigeration) and 1870s stone walls.

Of course, the trails here are worth visiting too. On the selected route, the Alambique and Bear Gulch Trails guide you through oaks, bay laurels, and redwoods as you visit three of the park's five "destination points": Alambique Flat and Redwood Flat (both redwood groves) and the Meadows, the park's only grassland (read about the other destination points in Go Farther). Deer are a common sight here, so keep an eye out. This park is popular, but it doesn't feel crowded. It's also mostly shaded, so it's a great pick even on warm days.

GET MOVING

From the parking lot, walk to the main stable and pick up the Alambique Trail (junction 6) on your left. (The Bear Gulch Trail also starts in the parking lot, so make sure you're taking the correct trail.) You'll be on the wide Alambique Trail for 2.3 miles.

Stay straight at junction 12, then continue another 0.7 mile to junction 16. Along this stretch, you will pass through your first redwood grove and can see Stanford's Hoover Tower off to the left. To stay on the Almabique Trial, veer left at junction 16 and go straight shortly after at junction 17.

Continue on the Alambique Trail for another 1.2 miles to reach Alambique Flat, elevation 1,230 feet (2 miles total). Take a left to head into a serene redwood grove. There's a bench here that makes a nice place for a break after the elevation gain. Come back to where you took this detour and continue on the Alambique Trail. Stay left as you pass the Oak Trail at junction 21 (2.1 miles).

At 2.3 miles, arrive at the Bear Gulch Trail (junction 20), where you'll turn right. You'll be on this trail for the remaining 2.5 miles.

Continue 0.3 mile to the Meadow Trail at junction 18 and the Meadows (elevation 1,430 feet). There's a bench here where you can take a break or just sit in the grass and enjoy the views of surrounding mountains. You are finally heading downhill!

Head left and pass through a gate between the trash cans and a bench. From here on out, the singletrack Bear Gulch Trail winds downhill through mixed forest. You'll see bay laurels, Douglas- firs, tan oaks, madrones, and chaparral. At 3.4 miles, stay straight on the Bear Gulch Trail when you pass the

Redwood Trail (junction 10). On your right is Redwood Flat, elevation 1,110 feet.

Over the next 1.2 miles, stay straight on the Bear Gulch Trail, passing junction 9 at 3.5 miles, junction 2 at 4.1 miles, and junction 8 at 4.5 miles. From there continue the final 0.2 mile, spotting 1870s stone walls, walking behind the main stable, and arriving at junction 7 and the parking lot.

GO FARTHER

Visit this park's other destination points: Salamander Flat and the Crossroads. Or visit the Folger Estate or the Carriage Room Museum (see the "Folger Stable Historic Site" page of the County of San Mateo website for current hours).

Next page: Wildflowers line the shaded Hamm's Gulch Trail in Windy Hill Open Space Preserve (Hike 15). (Photo: Katie Cook)

SKYLINE BOULEVARD

This sparsely populated corridor is home to several large parks with unique sights. Purisima Creek Redwoods Preserve hits the perfect balance between views and redwoods. El Corte de Madera Creek Preserve has redwood groves, a plane crash site and memorial, and a 50-foot-tall tafoni sandstone monolith you won't want to miss. Then there's upper La Honda Creek Open Space Preserve. This (free) permit-only park limits daily visitors, so if you like solitude, this is the spot for you. You'll hike redwood trails, visit the aptly named "Big Tree," an old-growth redwood, and take in views of the Santa Cruz Mountains.

Next, head to Windy Hill Open Space Preserve, where you'll climb the park's eponymous hill and enjoy panoramic views over the Peninsula and the ocean. Then you head south to two adjacent parks: Russian Ridge and Skyline Ridge Open Space Preserve. Russian Ridge has miles of grasslands and views up to Napa County on clear days. Skyline Ridge features a pond, a lake, and spectacular views of the Santa Cruz Mountains.

Two other parks right next to each other are Monte Bello Preserve and Los Trancos Open Space Preserve. Monte Bello's selected route takes you through grasslands to the top of Black Mountain and back down through serene, shaded trails. Los Trancos Open Space Preserve brings the geological history of the San Andreas Fault to life with a self-guided tour. This trail shines in the rainy season when seasonal creeks flow and waterfalls dot the park.

Lastly, Long Ridge Open Space Preserve is a peaceful, tree-covered route that's perfect on a hot day and features a clearing with striking views of mountains and the ocean—perfect for anything from a quick snack break to pondering the meaning of life and the universe.

12 Purisima Creek Redwoods Preserve

DISTANCE: 7.3 miles
ELEVATION GAIN: 1,780 feet
HIGH POINT: 2,030 feet
DIFFICULTY: Challenging
TIME: 3 hours and 30 minutes
FITNESS: Hikers, runners
FAMILY-FRIENDLY: Families can park at the lot off Higgins Canyon Road and explore the redwoods without all the mileage, descents, and ascents.
DOG-FRIENDLY: No
AMENITIES: Restrooms at the North Ridge parking area and halfway through the hike near the Higgins Canyon Road entrance
CONTACT: Midpeninsula Regional Open Space District
GPS: 37° 27' 1.4508" N, 122° 20' 19.932" W

GETTING THERE

Map to: Purisima Creek North Ridge Trailhead, 5050 El Camino Real, Los Altos. **Parking:** Free parking at the North Ridge parking area off Skyline Boulevard/State Route 35. There are forty-one standard spaces and two ADA spaces. Parking can fill up quickly, so come early or in the late afternoon after the morning hikers have left.

Can't decide on a hike with views or redwoods? At Purisima Creek Redwoods Preserve, you don't have to choose. On this loop route, you start at 2,000 feet and descend 1,500 feet on the North Ridge and Whittemore Gulch Trails through a mix of forested and exposed areas with views of the surrounding hills and the ocean. By the time you bottom out, you'll find yourself in Purisima Creek Canyon, alongside Purisima Creek and among towering redwoods, abundant ferns, and banana slugs. You'll return to the start on the Harkins Ridge Trail (part

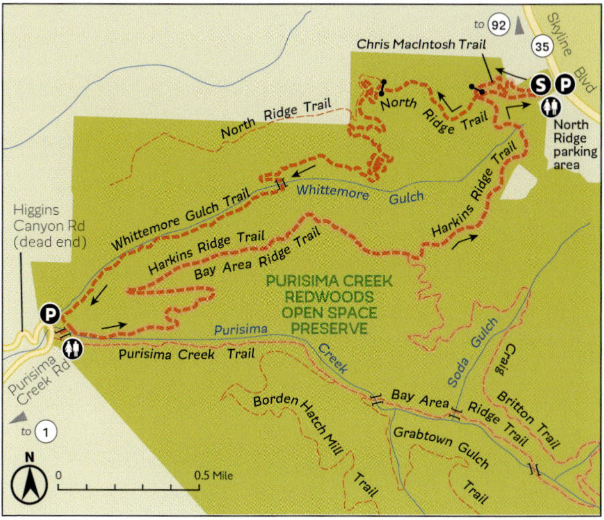

of the Bay Area Ridge Trail), again alternating between tree cover and views.

This hike has virtually no flat sections, so you'll be hiking down to the redwoods and straight back up. This write-up is for the counterclockwise route, but you can also go clockwise. Going counterclockwise means a longer and more gradual descent into the redwoods. Your ascent will be shorter but steeper.

GET MOVING

Walk through a gate to pick up the North Ridge Trail from the parking lot and head downhill. After 100 feet, pick up the hikers-only Chris MacIntosh Trail to the right. This trail is longer than the comparable segment of the North Ridge Trail by 0.2 mile, but its narrow tree-lined switchbacks are a pleasant way to ease into the hike.

Here you'll see Douglas-firs, a redwood or two, and moisture-loving plants like ferns. You'll get intermittent views

From the Chris MacIntosh Trail, you can spot the ocean and Pillar Point (Hike 5).

toward Pacifica's Montara Mountain and Half Moon Bay's Pillar Point (Hike 5). After half a mile, head through a fence and bear right at a four-way intersection to pick up the North Ridge Trail. On this stretch, there are some dramatic Douglas-firs.

At 1 mile, stay straight and walk through a gate to pick up the singletrack Whittemore Gulch Trail. On this switchbacked-filled trail, there are some more Douglas-firs, and you'll take in some lovely views of nearby hills and the ocean.

Descend 0.6 mile first through tree cover and then through chaparral, then make a hairpin turn left to stay on the Whittemore Gulch Trail. Descend for another 2.2 miles. After about half a mile into this stretch, you're solidly in the redwoods, and you'll see some large trees along the trail. At 2.8 miles, cross a bridge over Whittemore Gulch, where you continue downhill. As you head deeper into the redwoods, look for ferns, coastal hedgenettle, redwood sorrel, and banana slugs.

At 3.8 miles, reach a bridge where you stay straight to pick up the Harkins Ridge Trail. (There is a restroom across the bridge if you need it.) Just after this, you can take a break along Purisima Creek. This is a peaceful place to take in the redwoods, listen to the creek, and have a snack before you take on the 1,500-foot ascent back to the start.

When you're ready for your ascent, continue 0.4 mile and stay left at the "trail" sign. You'll soon climb out of the redwoods. You'll see Douglas-firs and chapparal as you make your way uphill. As you continue to climb, check out the westward views toward the ocean. You can also see the Whittemore Gulch Trail where you were earlier. Some sections here are steep, so pace yourself.

At the junction with the Craig Britton Trail at 6 miles, continue straight on the Harkins Ridge Trail. Then, at 6.3 miles, stay left on the Harkins Ridge Trail before you reach a preserve boundary sign. After this, you're on a singletrack trail. Continue until you reach a familiar four-way intersection at 7 miles. Turn right onto the wide North Ridge Trail and follow it back to the parking lot.

13 El Corte de Madera Creek Preserve

DISTANCE: 5.5 miles
ELEVATION GAIN: 1,130 feet
HIGH POINT: 2,320 feet
DIFFICULTY: Moderate
TIME: 2 hours and 30 minutes
FITNESS: Hikers, fit walkers, runners
FAMILY-FRIENDLY: Families or walkers looking for a shorter route can take the Tafoni Trail from the start of the hike and reach the sandstone formation in 1.3 miles.
DOG-FRIENDLY: No
AMENITIES: Picnic bench in the parking lot and at the vista point. Restrooms are at the parking area 1.2 miles south of Skeggs Point on State Route 35.
CONTACT: Midpeninsula Regional Open Space District
BEFORE YOU GO: You may want to bring hiking poles with you for the downhills here. Cyclists love these trails. Keep your eyes and ears open for fast-moving bikes.
GPS: 37° 24' 38.016" N, 122° 18' 22.968" W

GETTING THERE

Map to: Skeggs Point parking area, State Route 35, Redwood City. **Parking:** Free parking at Skeggs Point. The twenty-six spaces here (including one ADA space) can fill up early on weekends. Additional parking is available at a turnout 0.4 mile south of this, where you can use trails to reach the start of this route.

"El Corte de Madera" means "cutting wood," and this area was a logging site starting in the 1860s. The 2,908 acres became a preserve in 1988, and today you'll find 34 miles of multiuse trails shaded by tall second-growth redwoods and Douglas-firs.

On your loop through the park, you'll explore what makes it unique. El Corte de Madera was the site of a commercial plane crash in 1953. The plane, called *Resolution*, ended up in dense coastal fog on its approach to San Francisco

This 50-foot tall monolith took hundreds of thousands of years to form.

International Airport and crashed into the trees, killing all eight crew and eleven passengers aboard. Even decades later, some wreckage remains visible off the Resolution Trail. There is also a memorial to the crash off the Fir Trail.

You'll also visit a towering 50-foot-tall tafoni sandstone monolith. Tafoni are small, round hollows that develop in different types of rocks and take hundreds to thousands of years to form.

GET MOVING

From the Skeggs Point parking area, walk north on Skyline Boulevard. After 500 feet, cross the street carefully when you see a mailbox that reads "15006." A wood fence and informational signage mark the entrance to the preserve.

Pick up the Tafoni Trail, a wide dirt trail to your left, then stay right after 0.1 mile to pick up the El Corte de Madera Creek Trail. You'll be on this trail for a total of 2.3 miles. For most of the first mile, you'll descend over 400 feet through redwoods, Douglas-firs, and bay laurels along El Corte de Madera Creek. Toward the end of this stretch, you'll cross the creek using three bridges.

Once past the third bridge, you'll head mostly uphill for just under a mile. At a trail marker at the end of this stretch, stay right on the El Corte de Madera Creek Trail toward the Resolution Trail. Head downhill, losing 200 feet of elevation over the next 0.6 mile (until 2.4 miles total). When you get to a T, make a left onto the Resolution Trail.

You'll be on the Resolution Trail for a mile. At 0.3 mile into this trail, look for an easy-to-miss roped-off area where you can see some wreckage from the *Resolution* plane crash. Over the next 0.3 mile, the trail emerges from the tall trees to start a short rocky section lined with manzanita trees. At the end of this section, you'll arrive at a clearing and turn left on the Fir Trail. Stay on this trail until you reach the *Resolution* Aircraft Memorial. Just beyond the memorial, head uphill 350 feet to reach a vista point with a view of the ocean.

From the viewpoint, head back to the memorial and continue on the Fir Trail. At 3.9 miles, reach a four-way intersection. Turn left onto the Tafoni Trail, and shortly after, turn right to reach the sandstone formation and observation deck. Once there, read about the tafoni and gaze at the monolith on your right. Do not touch the sandstone!

When you're done, head back to the four-way intersection at 4.4 miles total. This time, take the tightest left for the Tafoni

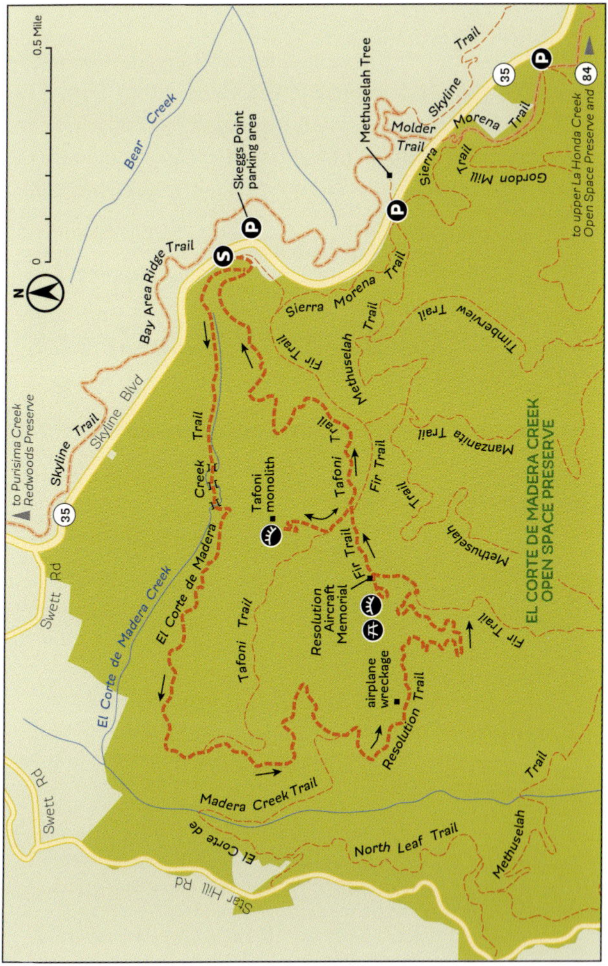

Trail to Skeggs Point. Continue on the Tafoni Trail for a mile. When the El Corte de Madera Creek Trail merges with the Tafoni Trail, continue back to where you entered the preserve and head back to Skeggs Point.

GO FARTHER

Visit the Methuselah Tree, the oldest and largest tree in the Santa Cruz Mountains outside Big Basin State Park. This 1,860-year-old redwood is 0.6 mile south of Skeggs Point. Look for another preserve entrance with a gate marked CM02 and a few parking spaces. Pull over, cross the street carefully, and walk 250 feet to visit this incredible tree!

14 Upper La Honda Creek Open Space Preserve

DISTANCE: 3.9 miles
ELEVATION GAIN: 780 feet
HIGH POINT: 2,210 feet
DIFFICULTY: Moderate
TIME: 1 hour and 45 minutes
FITNESS: Hikers, walkers, runners
FAMILY-FRIENDLY: Yes
DOG-FRIENDLY: Yes
AMENITIES: None
CONTACT: Midpeninsula Regional Open Space Park District
BEFORE YOU GO: You need a free permit to hike this route. Visit the "Permits" page of the Midpeninsula Regional Open Space Park District website to get one. When you receive your permit via email, you'll also receive a code to open the entrance gate lock. Give yourself a day or two to receive the permit after requesting it, and make sure to print the permit, as you'll need to display it on your car's dashboard. Because hiking is limited here, trails can become overgrown from disuse. You won't get lost on the overgrown trails, but you may want to wear long pants to protect yourself from ticks.
GPS: 37° 22' 40.8684" N, 122° 16' 44.6124" W

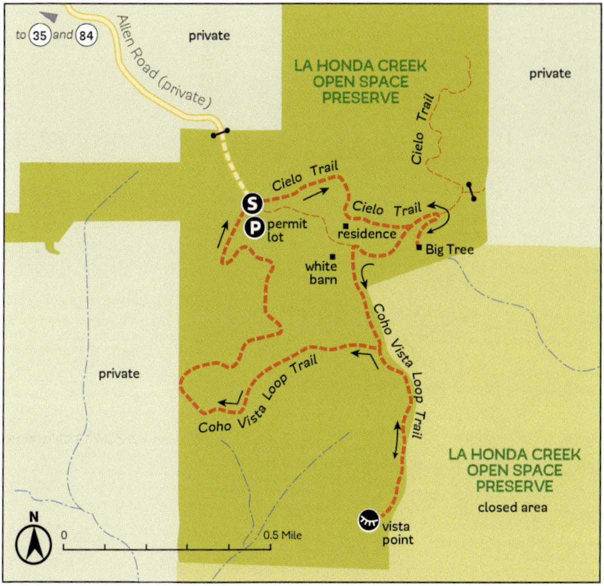

GETTING THERE

Map to: La Honda Creek at Allen Road permit lot. **Parking:** There is a small parking area at the start of the hike.

Come to upper La Honda Creek Open Space Preserve for peace, solitude, and views. Opened to the public in 2017, the park has expansive grasslands punctuated by shaded sections, which are a relief on hot days. Not only is there shade, but much of it comes from redwoods, including the "Big Tree," a giant old-growth redwood. In addition to the Big Tree, another highlight on the route is a viewpoint with 270-degree views of the Santa Cruz Mountains and the Pacific Ocean.

The selected route takes you on a loop encompassing most of the preserve's trails. You'll walk through a redwood grove, see the Big Tree, walk through grasslands hosting a

In La Honda Creek Open Space Preserve, you'll likely have these 270-degree views to yourself.

colorful display of wildflowers in spring, and head to the viewpoint. After the viewpoint, you'll enjoy a mix of grasslands and forest before you finish the hike.

GET MOVING

Pick up the Cielo Trail from the parking area. This wide, flat, shaded trail heads into redwoods and Douglas-firs. After half a mile, reach a junction at a small clearing in the trees. Stay straight here to complete a quick out-and-back detour to see the Big Tree. The turnoff for the Big Tree comes up on the right after 450 feet. Keep your eyes peeled, as the Cielo Trail keeps going and tall grasses may obscure the sign for the turnoff. On this 0.2-mile roundtrip detour, you'll descend and regain about 75 feet. You'll know the Big Tree when you see it!

After gawking at nature's majesty, return to the junction at the clearing (1 mile total). This time, you'll head left and uphill toward the Coho Vista Loop Trail. This is a wide fire trail like the Cielo Trail, but it gets more sun because oaks line the trail, not just redwoods and firs.

At 1.2 miles, exit the wooded area and see a private home on your right and a garage and a white barn on your left. As you reach Allen Road (paved), turn left to pick up the Coho Vista Loop Trail. When you reach a trail sign at 1.5 miles, stay straight on the Coho Vista Loop Trail to continue to the vista point. This stretch to the vista point is 1 mile roundtrip, and you'll lose 200 feet of elevation and regain it on the way back.

As you head to the vista point, just over a quarter mile through this stretch, leave the grassy trails and duck back into a redwood grove. There are some larger trees to your left as you enter the grove. As you emerge from the redwoods, you'll see a sign that says you're 0.1 mile from the vista point.

When you reach the vista point at 2 miles, you'll get 270-degree views of the Santa Cruz Mountains. When you've had your fill, head half a mile back to the trail marker that says the parking lot is 1.4 miles away, and make a left to continue on the Coho Vista Loop Trail. After a short initial ascent, you'll descend through grasslands for almost half a mile and then climb 275 feet over 1 mile of oak woodlands, redwoods, and Douglas-firs back to the start.

GO FARTHER

Visit the trails of lower La Honda Creek Preserve, including the easy-access Grasshopper Trail, which opened in June 2022. This trail is designed to show hikers some of the best aspects of this park in just over a mile, including grasslands, oak woodlands, redwoods, and viewpoints. It is named for two species that live in the grasslands found here: the grasshopper and the grasshopper sparrow.

15 Windy Hill Open Space Preserve

DISTANCE: 7.6 miles
ELEVATION GAIN: 1,540 feet
HIGH POINT: 1,905 feet
DIFFICULTY: Challenging
TIME: 3 hours
FITNESS: Hikers, walkers, runners. Walkers and families with younger children can park in one of the two lots on Skyline Boulevard for a shorter hike to Windy Hill.
FAMILY-FRIENDLY: See above.
DOG-FRIENDLY: Yes
AMENITIES: Restrooms, water, benches, picnic areas, overlooks
CONTACT: Midpeninsula Regional Open Space District
GPS: 37° 22' 31.5912" N, 122° 13' 23.6892" W

GETTING THERE

Map to: 555 Portola Road, Portola Valley. **Public Transit:** SamTrans bus 87 stops at Portola Road and Grove Drive, a 0.2-mile walk from the hike start/end (weekdays only). **Parking:** Free parking. The Lower Windy Hill parking area has forty-seven spaces and two ADA spaces. Overflow parking is available at the Portola Valley Town Center, 0.4 mile north on Portola Road.

Named for its breezy summit, Portola Valley's Windy Hill Open Space Preserve is a prime place to take in Bay Area views. You'll use the Hamms Gulch Trail to take a long but gradual ascent through shaded woodlands. You'll then exit the woods to reach a ridge with views across the Peninsula and Bay. You'll summit two neighboring hilltops to reach the Herb Grench Overlook and Windy Hill, both with 360-degree views. Then, you'll descend on the Spring Ridge Trail, hiking through expansive grasslands and chaparral environments.

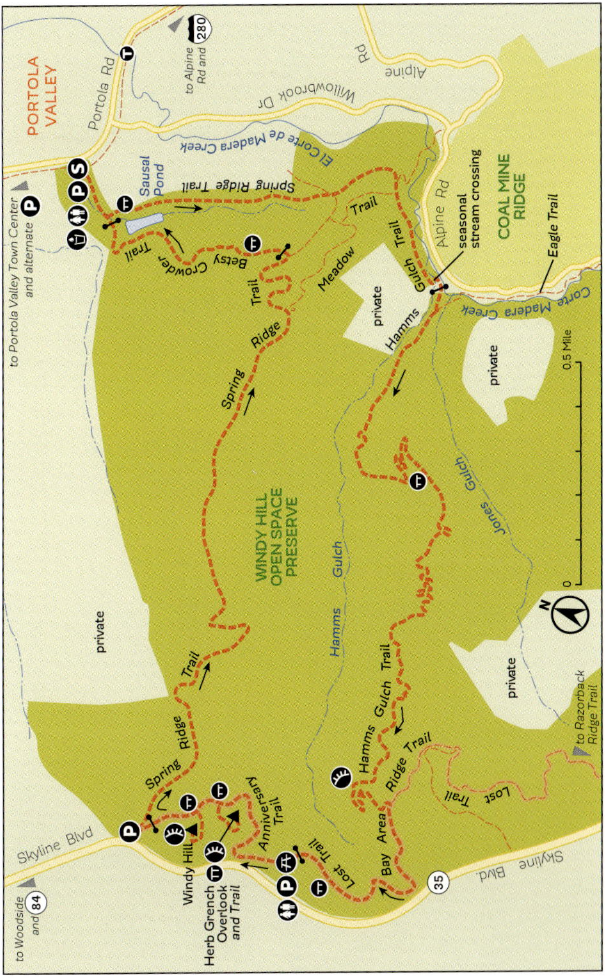

This park is a winner in spring, as it's known for its vibrant wildflower displays. And you'll want to visit on a clear day to make the most of the expansive views up to San Francisco, down to Mountain View, and across the Bay to the Diablo

Range. These trails are dog-friendly, so bring your furry friend, and don't forget a lunch or snack to give you a reason to linger atop Windy Hill.

GET MOVING

Pick up the Spring Ridge Trail, a wide fire trail, behind the restroom in the parking lot. After 250 feet, turn left to stay on the Spring Ridge Trail, where you'll walk between a retirement community and Sausal Pond. Stay on this oak-lined trail for half a mile to arrive at a meadow. Cross the meadow and continue straight toward the Hamms Gulch Trail, then pass a four-way intersection at 0.8 mile. In 100 feet, head right toward Hamms Gulch, and 175 feet later stay left to pick up the Hamms Gulch Trail. You'll be on the Hamms Gulch Trail for 2.7 miles until you reach the Lost Trail.

The Spring Ridge Trail shines in springtime when green grass and wildflowers line the trails.

Head uphill on the narrow trail lined with redwoods, oaks, bay laurels, and poison oak. At 1.1 miles, cross a seasonal creek. Soon after, head straight through a gate. At 1.9 miles, reach a bench at a tight switchback where you can see the Herb Grench Overlook and Windy Hill. Starting on this stretch, you'll get views of Mount Diablo and other Diablo Range mountains, including Mission and Monument Peak.

At 3.3 miles, head right at a T to visit a viewpoint 100 feet down the trail. You'll get views of Mount Diablo, the Bay, Stanford University, and the Stanford Dish (Hike 22). Head back to the Hamms Gulch Trail, and after 0.3 mile, head right at a switchback to pick up the Lost Trail (also part of the Bay Area Ridge Trail).

Follow the Lost Trail until 4.2 miles total to reach a parking area with a restroom and picnic benches. You now pick up the Anniversary Trail. After 0.2 mile, pass through a gate and stay right on the Anniversary Trail. As you climb uphill through expansive grasslands, enjoy your first glimpses of the ocean.

At 4.6 miles, arrive at two benches. Head left and behind them to visit the Herb Grench Overlook (Herb Grench was the first general manager of the Midpeninsula Regional Open Space District). From this summit, you can see San Francisco to the north and Shoreline Amphitheatre to the southeast, in addition to the views you saw earlier. When you're done enjoying the panorama, head back to the Anniversary Trail. At 4.8 miles, reach a bench where you'll head left and uphill to the summit of Windy Hill (1,905 feet), the highest point on this route. Here you'll see the same sights from the Herb Grench Overlook—just from slightly higher up.

Return to the Anniversary Trail. At 5.1 miles, reach two gates and another parking area, then head right. You're now leaving the Bay Area Ridge Trail and picking up the Spring Ridge Trail, a wide fire trail. Enjoy an uninterrupted 1.5-mile stretch through grasslands and chaparral with no junctions.

At 6.6 miles, stay straight on the Spring Ridge Trail. Shortly after this, you head into the woods. After 0.3 mile, turn left to pick up the Betsy Crowder Trail. Pass through a gate, then walk alongside Sausal Pond. You'll be on this trail for a little over half a mile. Pass through a gate, and when you reach a T, turn left to head back to the parking lot.

16 Russian Ridge Open Space Preserve

DISTANCE: 4.9 miles
ELEVATION GAIN: 850 feet
HIGH POINT: 2,572 feet
DIFFICULTY: Moderate
TIME: 2 hours
FITNESS: Hikers, walkers, runners
FAMILY-FRIENDLY: Families and walkers can opt for a short hike to Borel Hill and back.
DOG-FRIENDLY: No
AMENITIES: Restroom, benches
CONTACT: Midpeninsula Regional Open Space District
BEFORE YOU GO: This preserve is best on clear days in spring when the grass is green and the wildflowers are out. The parking lot can fill up quickly during wildflower season.
GPS: 37° 18' 53.8596" N, 122° 11' 18.7512" W

GETTING THERE

Map to: Russian Ridge Preserve parking, 3901 Alpine Road, La Honda. **Parking:** Free parking with thirty-seven standard spaces and two ADA spaces.

Russian Ridge was named for Mr. Paskey, a Russian immigrant who grazed cattle and ran a dairy farm here from

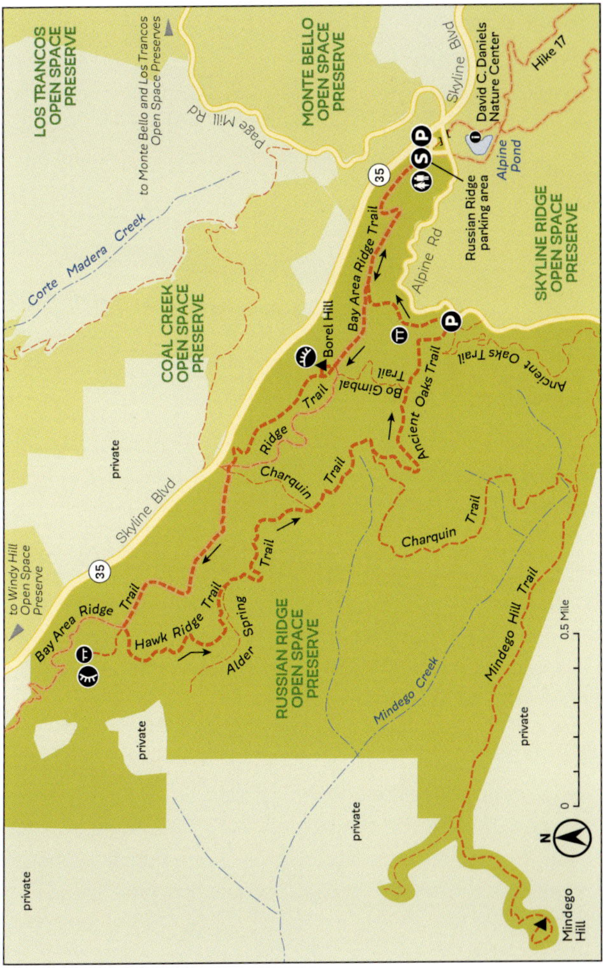

roughly 1920 to 1950. The ridge where this 3,137-acre park sits boasts some of the best views in the Bay Area. To the east, you'll see the Peninsula and the Diablo Range. To the

Ridgeline trails with sweeping views are a common sight in Russian Ridge Open Space Preserve.

west, you'll look toward the ocean. To the south, you'll see the Santa Cruz Mountains, and to the north, you'll get views of San Francisco and even Napa on clear days. One of the best places to take in these views is 2,572-foot-tall Borel Hill, which you reach 0.8 mile into this route.

You'll take the Ridge Trail for your outbound journey and then several other trails to complete this large loop. You'll spend most of your time in grasslands, but will enjoy some intermittent shade on the second half of the route. Russian Ridge reaches peak beauty on clear days during wildflower season, but that's also when you'll encounter peak crowds.

GET MOVING

Pick up the Bay Area Ridge Trail from the parking lot and head uphill through grasslands. As you climb, you'll get views of Mount Diablo and the Diablo Range. At 0.6 mile, continue straight on the Ridge Trail as a trail branches off to the left. You'll end up back at this intersection at the end of the hike.

Continue for 0.2 mile and stay straight on an unnamed trail as the Ridge Trail bears left. In 100 feet, climb a dirt trail on the right to the summit of Borel Hill. On a clear day, you can see San Francisco, Mount Tamalpais in Marin, and even Mount St. Helena in Napa to the north. To the northeast, you can see the Peninsula, Stanford's campus, and the Diablo Range. To the northwest, you can see the ocean, and closer in, Mindego Hill, a hill in this preserve that's half carpeted in grass and half covered in trees.

Head downhill to continue on the unnamed trail you were on before. You're now at 0.8 mile total. At 1.3 miles, reach a four-way intersection and head straight to rejoin the Ridge Trail. From here, look left to see Mindego Hill from closer up.

You reach another four-way intersection at 2 miles. If you'd like a break here, continue straight for a short out-and-back detour to a bench looking toward the ocean (not included in route mileage). If you're not taking a break here, make a left at this intersection to pick up the Hawk Ridge Trail, a singletrack trail through grasslands. The ridge rises up to your left and views of Mindego Hill, the ocean, and the Santa Cruz Mountains are on your right.

At 2.6 miles, continue straight onto the Alder Spring Trail. On this stretch, you walk through a mix of grasslands and oak woodlands and get closer-up views of Mindego Hill. At 3 miles, reach a T where you head right on the Charquin Trail toward the Ancient Oaks Trail. Head through a mix of grasslands and oaks.

At 3.3 miles, head left and steeply uphill on the shaded Ancient Oaks Trail. Continue uphill for half a mile. The Bo Gimbal Trail branches off to your left at 3.7 miles, but stay straight here to enjoy a dramatic section where you can see the trail winding in front of you through the grasslands. At 4.1 miles, turn left, and in 0.4 mile, arrive at the Ridge Trail. Turn right and continue downhill to the start.

GO FARTHER

Hike to the top of Mindego Hill for a 4.6-mile out-and-back route with 1,300 feet of elevation gain. At the summit, you'll be treated to mountain and ocean views.

17 Skyline Ridge Open Space Preserve

DISTANCE: 4.3 miles
ELEVATION GAIN: 770 feet
HIGH POINT: 2,490 feet
DIFFICULTY: Moderate
TIME: 1 hour and 30 minutes
FITNESS: Hikers, walkers, runners. Walkers should note the 500 feet in elevation gain in the second half of the hike.
FAMILY-FRIENDLY: Families can do a hike around Alpine Pond, have a picnic, and visit the David C. Daniels Nature Center.
DOG-FRIENDLY: No
AMENITIES: Restrooms, benches, picnic area, water, nature center overlook
CONTACT: Midpeninsula Regional Open Space District
BEFORE YOU GO: Go on a clear day to make the most of the views. The parking lot can fill up quickly during wildflower season.
GPS: 37° 18' 53.8596" N, 122° 11' 18.7512" W

GETTING THERE

Map to: Russian Ridge Preserve parking, 3901 Alpine Road, La Honda. **Parking:** Free parking with thirty-seven standard spaces and two ADA spaces.

Skyline Ridge Open Space Preserve and Russian Ridge Open Space Preserve (Hike 16) are so proximate they share a parking lot, but they each have special things to offer. What makes Skyline Ridge stand out is its interpretive center, two bodies of

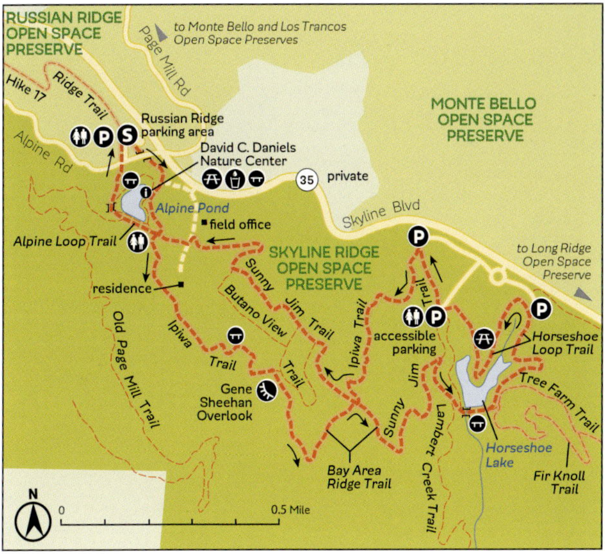

water, many miles on the Bay Area Ridge Trail, and sweeping mountain views.

A highlight of this route is the Ipiwa Trail, which you'll take from Alpine Pond and the David C. Daniels Nature Center to the Gene Sheehan Overlook, where you'll enjoy magnificent views of the Santa Cruz Mountains. From here, you'll take the Sunny Jim Trail down to flat and peaceful Horseshoe Lake. ("Sunny Jim" refers to James Rolph, Jr., who once owned this land and served as the mayor of San Francisco and later as the governor of California.) After circling the lake, you'll ascend 500 feet and then head back to the start on a combination of the Ipiwa and Sunny Jim Trails.

GET MOVING

From the Russian Ridge parking lot, descend a stairway and walk through a culvert to cross Alpine Road. Once on the other side, you're on the Ipiwa Trail. Reach a picnic area at 0.2 mile,

Horseshoe Lake is one of two bodies of water on this route through Skyline Ridge.

then shortly after, reach the David C. Daniels Nature Center and Alpine Pond. Continue past the nature center. When the trail splits, take the left fork to continue on the Ipiwa Trail.

At 0.2 mile, continue straight at a four-way intersection to stay on the Ipiwa Trail toward Horseshoe Lake. Continue on the Ipiwa Trail for a mile. You'll hike uphill and downhill through several environments, including oak and bay laurel woodlands, grasslands, and chaparral with manzanita. Halfway through this stretch, you'll reach the Gene Sheehan Overlook, which features panoramic views of the Santa Cruz Mountains and the Pacific Ocean. And in the last 0.2 mile, look for Monte Bello Preserve's Black Mountain ahead and in the distance (look for the tower atop the hill).

At 1.2 miles, head right at a four-way intersection to pick up the Sunny Jim Trail. From here, you can see Loma Prieta and Mount Umunhum in the distance. Head downhill through grasslands and chaparral. At 1.6 miles, take a sharp right at a trail sign to turn away from Skyline parking and toward the

Horseshoe Loop Trail. When the trail splits about 0.1 mile after this, stay left toward a bridge and the Horseshoe Loop Trail. You'll be on this trail for 1 mile.

On this stretch, ignore turnoffs for the Tree Farm Trail after 0.1 mile, a parking lot after another 0.4 mile, and another parking lot after an additional 0.5 mile. At that second lot, cross the road to pick up the Sunny Jim Trail. Then continue to a third parking lot, where you pick up the Ipiwa Trail (2.8 miles total).

Head uphill, gaining 300 feet and crossing through chaparral and oak woodlands. During the rainy season, you may pass by seasonal streams and waterfalls. After half a mile, reach the four-way intersection you encountered at 1.2 miles. This time, head right on the Sunny Jim Trail. There are many lovely old oak trees on this stretch. You'll pass two junctions for the Butano View Trail (which you can explore but is not included in route mileage). At the second junction, you'll start heading downhill.

After half a mile, turn right to stay on the Sunny Jim Trail at a third junction with the Butano View Trail. Then follow the trail as it bends left and meets up with a paved road at 4 miles total. Turn left on the road and then take a jog right to continue on the Sunny Jim Trail. You are now heading downhill through more oak woodlands.

At 4.1 miles, continue straight through the four-way intersection that you crossed by Alpine Pond near the start of the hike. Then shortly after this, you reach a restroom on your left, with two trails in front of you and one to the right. Of the two trails in front of you, take the one on the right that runs along Alpine Pond. Follow the trail as it bends right; when the trail splits after a bridge, stay left. Cross Alpine Road and soon reach the parking area.

GO FARTHER

Visit Russian Ridge Open Space Preserve across the street (Hike 16).

18 Monte Bello Open Space Preserve

DISTANCE: 6 miles
ELEVATION GAIN: 1,240 feet
HIGH POINT: 2,800 feet
DIFFICULTY: Challenging
TIME: 2 hours
FITNESS: Hikers, runners
FAMILY-FRIENDLY: This route is best for families with older children due to the elevation gain.
DOG-FRIENDLY: No
ACCESSIBLE: No
AMENITIES: Restrooms, benches, pay phone, campsite
CONTACT: Midpeninsula Regional Open Space District
GPS: 37° 19' 32.9988" N, 122° 10' 44.814" W

GETTING THERE

Map to: 4301 Page Mill Road, Los Altos. **Parking:** Free parking with fifty-one standard spaces and four ADA spaces. Additional free parking with twenty-three standard spaces and one ADA space across Page Mill Road at Los Trancos Open Space Preserve.

This 6-mile loop around Monte Bello Open Space Preserve takes you to Black Mountain's rocky summit for sweeping mountain views. In the late 1800s and early 1900s, this area was the site of Back Mountain Ranch, Stevens Creek Road Ranch, and Monte Bello Ranch. Black Mountain and the Black Mountain Backpack Camp you pass on this route (the only campsite in the Midpeninsula Regional Open Space District) are named for the old Black Mountain Ranch.

As you might expect with ranchland, many trails here pass through open grasslands. These grasslands are lovely and green in spring but can be hot in summer. If you hike in

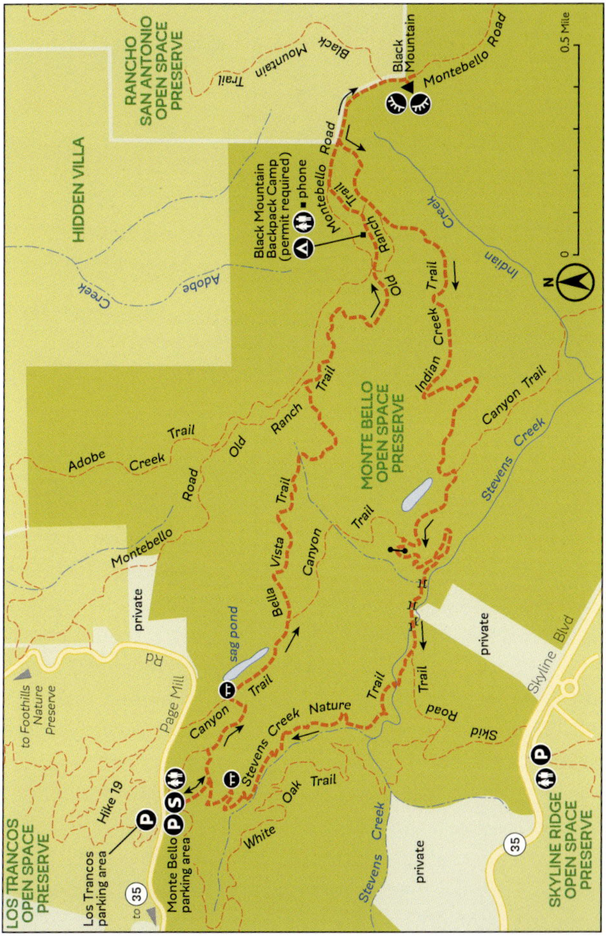

summer, know that you'll have shade for the last 2 miles of the route. But keep in mind also that you'll still need to save some energy for the end: You'll gain 400 feet of elevation on this hike's last mile.

This collection of rocks marks the top of Black Mountain in Monte Bello Open Space Preserve.

GET MOVING

Pick up the Stevens Creek Nature Trail by the informational signage in the parking area. Take this trail 450 feet, then turn left toward the Canyon Trail. You'll find yourself surrounded by grasslands with mountains in the distance. After another 400 feet, turn right. You can now see Black Mountain looming above and to the left. After 0.1 mile, follow the "trail" sign left. When you reach a junction for the Canyon Trail, turn right toward the Backpack Camp.

Here, you'll walk along a "sag pond," a sunken area that filled with water from an underground spring after some fault movement (this preserve lies on the San Andreas Fault). After 0.2 mile on the Canyon Trail (0.6 mile total), head left and uphill on the Bella Vista Trail. This narrow singletrack trail climbs through grasslands shaded by the very occasional oak tree.

Stay on the Bella Vista Trail for 0.8 mile until you merge with the Old Ranch Trail. On this stretch, you'll see views of the Peninsula off to your right, and you may hear car noise from State Route 35. Stay on the Old Ranch Trail for half a mile. At

1.9 miles, Montebello Road is on your left and the singletrack Old Ranch Trail is on your right. Here you'll stay in the middle to head toward the Backpack Camp.

At 2 miles, walk through Black Mountain Backpack Camp, which has a restroom and a working pay phone. Follow the fire road as it bears left. Views soon open up to the left, and you'll see the Stanford Dish (Hike 22) and Stanford's Hoover Tower. At 2.2 miles, you'll join up with Montebello Road.

Stay on Montebello Road, walking past some radio towers. Ignore a trail that comes in from the left at the towers. At 2.5 miles, you're at the top of Black Mountain (elevation 2,812 feet) with a nice view of Mount Umunhum. A rocky area to the right is a great place to have a lunch break!

After taking in the views, backtrack on Montebello Road for 0.2 mile, then turn left on the Indian Creek Trail, a wide fire road. At 2.9 miles, when the trail splits again, bear left and head downhill to stay on the Indian Creek Trail. Descend steeply for a full mile. When the trail splits, turn right on the Canyon Trail toward Monte Bello Parking in 1.4 miles. Then in about a quarter mile, after a flat grassy area on the left, make a left and head slightly downhill, following a sign for Monte Bello Parking in 1.8 miles (don't worry—despite these signs, you are getting closer to the end of this route). You are now on the Stevens Creek Nature Trail. In 200 feet, go through a gate. You'll descend through bay laurels and oaks and then walk next to and over Stevens Creek, crossing several bridges along the way.

At 4.8 miles, turn right to stay on the Stevens Creek Nature Trail toward Monte Bello Parking in 1.2 miles. Over the next 1.1 miles, you'll gain 400 feet of elevation as you take gradual switchbacks uphill. Then head left and hike the final stretch to reach the parking lot where you started.

GO FARTHER

Check out Los Trancos Open Space Preserve (Hike 19) directly across Page Mill Road.

19 Los Trancos Open Space Preserve

DISTANCE: 3.1 miles
ELEVATION GAIN: 580 feet
HIGH POINT: 2,220 feet
DIFFICULTY: Moderate
TIME: 1 hour and 30 minutes
FITNESS: Hikers, walkers, runners
FAMILY-FRIENDLY: Yes, families can return to the start after the Nonette Hanko San Andreas Fault Trail.
DOG-FRIENDLY: No
AMENITIES: Restroom in Monte Bello parking area across Page Mill Road, benches, interpretive trail
CONTACT: Midpeninsula Regional Open Space District
BEFORE YOU GO: Before you hike, pick up a brochure in the parking lot with information on the Nonette Hanko San Andreas Fault Trail. In case there are no brochures at the lot, you can also print the hike guide from the "Los Trancos Preserve" page of the Midpeninsula Regional Open Space District website.
GPS: 37° 19' 34.2228" N, 122° 10' 46.4916" W

GETTING THERE

Map to: Los Trancos Open Space Preserve. **Parking:** Free parking with twenty-three standard spaces and one ADA space. Additional free parking with fifty-one standard spaces and four ADA spaces across Page Mill Road at Monte Bello Open Space Preserve.

Los Trancos Open Space Preserve straddles San Mateo and Santa Clara Counties, and it also sits upon the San Andreas Fault, dividing the American and Pacific Plates. On the first half of this route, you'll immerse yourself in fault history with a self-guided tour of the San Andreas Fault Trail. The nine-station trail was created in 1977 with

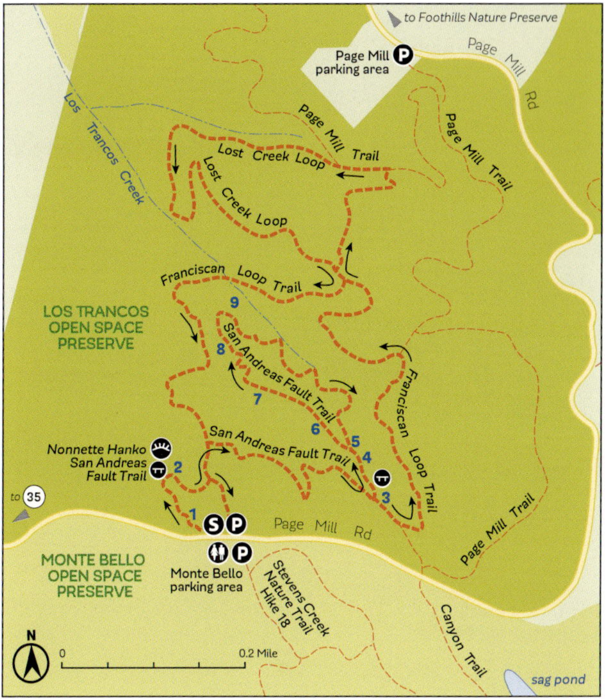

help from former Foothill College geology professor Tim Hall and his students.

The second half of the route takes you on the Lost Creek and Franciscan Loop Trails. All but the very start and end of the route are shaded, and there's just one view over the Peninsula on the entire hike. You'll be grateful for the shade in summer when neighboring parks are sweltering. The best time to hike here, however, is during the rainy season, when streams and waterfalls crop up throughout the preserve. Note: Beginner hikers should conserve their energy; over half the route's elevation comes in the last mile of this hike.

This section of San Andreas Fault Trail illustrates how a fence might have been broken in the aftermath of the 1906 earthquake.

GET MOVING

From the west side Los Trancos parking lot (away from the informational signage), pick up a singletrack trail heading uphill. This is the Nonette Hanko San Andreas Fault Trail (hereafter referred to as the San Andreas Fault Trail). Hanko was part of a group of people who worked to create the Midpeninsula Regional Open Space District. She also spent forty-six years on the district's board of directors.

If you have a San Andreas Fault Trail brochure, you can start reading along at station 1. At 0.1 mile, you reach station 2, where there is a bench and you can enjoy the only view toward the Peninsula and South Bay on this route. Turn right, then follow the trail sign right.

Follow the next trail sign left. Then at 0.2 mile, head straight to continue on the San Andreas Fault Trail. At 0.5 mile, reach station 3 where you take a sharp left toward a bench to stay on the San Andreas Fault Trail. You'll quickly arrive at station

4, which has a reproduction of a broken fence, symbolizing what a fence could have looked like after the 1906 earthquake when the ground shifted several feet in places.

Stay left at the next San Andreas Fault Trail sign to visit the remaining stations on a 0.5-mile clockwise loop. You are now in woods replete with oak and bay laurel trees. It can get damp here during the rainy season, and seasonal streams and small waterfalls may crop up along the trail. When you finish the loop at 1 mile total, make a left and head through the broken fence and back to station 3. Then, at 1.2 miles, make a sharp left to follow a sign for the Franciscan Loop Trail to the Lost Creek Loop Trail. Head gently downhill, then enjoy a nice flat stretch lined with tall bay laurels.

At 1.4 miles, continue straight on the Franciscan Loop Trail toward the Lost Creek Trail. You're now hiking through moss-covered oaks and bay laurels alongside a seasonal stream. After 0.2 mile, pass a turnoff for the Franciscan Loop Trail; then at the trail sign just ahead of you, turn right on the Lost Creek Loop Trail in the direction of the Page Mill Trail.

At 1.8 miles, head left on the Page Mill Trail. You may see a seasonal waterfall here, and you'll walk alongside a seasonal stream. A few hundred feet after this, stay straight to pick up the Lost Creek Loop Trail again. On this stretch, you may come across another seasonal waterfall. At 2 miles, as you near Los Trancos Creek, you may want to pace yourself, as you'll be gaining close to 400 feet of elevation on the last mile of this hike.

Finish the Lost Creek Loop at 2.5 miles. Head straight at a trail sign, then turn right at the trail sign just ahead to pick up the Franciscan Loop Trail toward the Page Mill parking area. After half a mile (3 miles total), turn right at a T. Then follow the trail sign straight and back to the parking lot.

GO FARTHER

Head across the street for a hike at Monte Bello Open Space Preserve (Hike 18).

20 Long Ridge Open Space Preserve

DISTANCE:	4.6 miles
ELEVATION GAIN:	650 feet
HIGH POINT:	2,510 feet
DIFFICULTY:	Moderate
TIME:	2 hours
FITNESS:	Hikers, walkers
FAMILY-FRIENDLY:	Yes, families can turn around at the pond for a 3-mile hike, but they will miss the ridge views.
DOG-FRIENDLY:	Dog-friendly for the first 0.4 mile of this route. People who want to hike with dogs can do a different route, turning right on the Chestnut Trail after 0.4 mile.
AMENITIES:	Bench at a viewpoint
CONTACT:	Midpeninsula Regional Open Space District
BEFORE YOU GO:	No restrooms are available on this route.
GPS:	37° 17' 24.5544" N, 122° 9' 14.868" W

GETTING THERE

Map to: Peters Creek Trailhead, La Honda. **Parking:** Free parking is available along Skyline Boulevard/State Route 35 at the Peters Creek and Grizzly Flat parking areas. There are also spaces across the street at Upper Stevens Creek County Park.

This route in Long Ridge Open Space Preserve drops you from busy Skyline Boulevard onto the serene Peters Creek Trail, where you'll enjoy a walk along a pond and creek through a wooded landscape full of moss-covered trees. From the creek, you'll gradually climb to Long Ridge Road, where you exit the woods. On this stretch, you reach a bench and viewpoint with views of the Santa Cruz Mountains and ocean. You'll head back to the start on the Long Ridge Trail, which features more forested trails, a large rock formation, and a steep descent.

Most of this route is forested, so it can be a shady escape on hot days. And during the rainy season, the Peters Creek and Long Ridge Trails are closed to cyclists and horses. While hikers will have the trails to themselves, they may also have to contend with muddy trail conditions.

GET MOVING

From the parking area, pick up the singletrack Peters Creek Trail. You'll be on this trail for 2.1 miles until the intersection of Long Ridge Road and Ward Road.

After a short walk, dip into the woods. At 0.4 mile, head left at a T to stay on the Peters Creek Trail toward the Long Ridge Trail. You are now on the Bay Area Ridge Trail. At 0.5 mile, continue straight on the Peters Creek Trail and walk along Peters Creek, which can be full of rushing water during and shortly after the rainy season.

Santa Cruz Mountain views are abundant between Long Ridge Road and the start of the Long Ridge Trail. (Photo: Tikva Morowati)

At 0.9 mile, continue straight on the Peters Creek Trail, then 0.3 mile later continue straight again (the trail to your left exits the park). Continue an additional 0.4 mile on the Peters Creek Trail. At the end of this stretch, the trail narrows as you approach Two Moon Lake and a bridge.

Over the next half a mile (until 2.1 miles total), you'll climb around 180 feet up gentle switchbacks to reach the intersection of Long Ridge Road and Ward Road. (There are actual street signs here!)

Make a right onto Long Ridge Road and exit the trees, leaving the Bay Area Ridge Trail. You'll be on a wide fire road that passes through grasslands and offers views to the east and west.

Continue half a mile to arrive at a bench and an overlook with views of the Santa Cruz Mountains and the ocean on clear days. This bench is dedicated to the memory of Pulitzer Prize–winning author Wallace Stegner, an environmentalist and a supporter of the Midpeninsula Regional Open Space District.

After exploring the overlook, pick up the Long Ridge Trail, where you'll hike for the next 1.5 miles. The first 0.8 mile of this trail descends through the woods, with a sharper descent during the second half. Toward the end of this stretch, look for a tall, moss-covered rock formation on your left.

At an intersection at 3.4 miles, follow an arrow in front of a gate to stay on the trail. Continue on the Long Ridge Trail for another 0.7 mile (until 4.1 miles total). Head uphill, and a little over a quarter mile into this stretch, look for a small trail sign. Soon, you'll start descending steeply through Douglas-firs to reach Peters Creek. At 4.1 miles, reach your original junction with the Peters Creek Trail. Turn left and walk a half mile back to where you started.

GO FARTHER

Hike the Hickory Oaks Trail to visit the preserve's two other hilltop benches. Or head across the street to visit the forested trails of Upper Stevens Creek County Park.

Next page: This viewpoint at Foothills Nature Preserve (Hike 23) has views of the Peninsula, Bay, and Diablo Range.

SOUTHERN PENINSULA

Heading down the Peninsula from where the Midpeninsula chapter left off, this chapter aims to get you outside in areas often better known for their technology than their nature. By hiking all the routes in this chapter, you'll explore the wilder side of Silicon Valley.

This chapter kicks off with three routes in Palo Alto. Pearson-Arastradero Preserve has expansive grasslands and views on trails that many animals call home. The Stanford Dish, a paved, accessible route over rolling hills, is a Bay Area classic. And Foothills Nature Preserve has only been open to the public since 2020—you won't want to miss the deer, the sights from Vista Hill, and tranquil Boronda Lake.

Next, you have two bayside hikes: Baylands Nature Preserve and the Sunnyvale Bay Trail. Both routes are flat, accessible, and rich with bird-watching opportunities. As a bonus, they're dog-friendly too.

With six often-full parking lots, Rancho San Antonio is a fitness mainstay for those in and around Los Altos. You can take a short, flat walk to Deer Hollow Farm or continue to higher elevations with scenic views.

Lastly, there are three side-by-side parks in Cupertino. Farthest west is Picchetti Ranch Open Space Preserve, where you can hike the Zinfandel Trail before enjoying a picnic and a wine tasting. Then there's Stevens Creek County Park, where you'll follow a short and pleasant route near a large reservoir. Farthest east is Fremont Older Open Space Preserve, where you'll hike through expansive grasslands to two hilltops offering panoramic views over the Santa Clara Valley.

21 Enid W. Pearson-Arastradero Preserve

DISTANCE: 4.1 miles
ELEVATION GAIN: 580 feet
HIGH POINT: 740 feet
DIFFICULTY: Moderate
TIME: 2 hours
FITNESS: Hikers, walkers, runners
FAMILY-FRIENDLY: Yes
DOG-FRIENDLY: Yes, on leash
AMENITIES: Restrooms, visitor center, water, benches, picnic tables
CONTACT: City of Palo Alto
BEFORE YOU GO: Some trails on this route close seasonally due to rain. Check trail statuses on the "Pearson-Arastradero Preserve" page of the City of Palo Alto website before heading out.
GPS: 37° 23' 13.8084" N, 122° 10' 29.0532" W

GETTING THERE

Map to: Pearson-Arastradero Preserve parking, 1530 Arastradero Road, Palo Alto. **Parking:** Plentiful free parking.

Enid W. Pearson was a Palo Alto resident who fought to preserve and develop local parks, and her namesake Enid W. Pearson-Arastradero Preserve is a kid-, bike-, and dog-friendly fitness wonderland with lots of trails to explore. Animals abound here, so watch out for horses, horse poop, and coyotes, which can all be common sights. The selected route highlights the park's wooded and grassland trails south of Arastradero Road and offers sweeping eastward views of the Stanford Dish (Hike 22), the Diablo Range, and the Bay.

Note: Certain trails in this park (including some on this route) close seasonally due to rain. If you want to hike here

during the rainy season, be sure to check the trail status online before you hike. If trails are closed when you visit, you can still enjoy the preserve. I note a rainy season detour below.

An impressive oak tree and a bench greet you at the viewpoint. (Photo: Yasaman Mohsenin)

GET MOVING

From the parking lot, head to the visitor center and take the trail past the restrooms. When you reach Arastradero Road, cross at the crosswalk. In 150 feet, stay straight on the Juan Bautista de Anza Trail (hereafter referred to as the de Anza Trail), a wide gravel trail lined with oaks. At 0.2 mile make a right on the Meadowlark Trail, which brings you into grasslands.

At 0.3 mile, turn left to stay on the Meadowlark Trail. Stay left when the trail splits after a quarter mile. Then, continue 0.1 mile to a four-way intersection, where you turn right on the de Anza Trail. At 0.8 mile, pick up the singletrack Ohlone Trail on the left. Remain here for 0.2 mile. (If seasonal closures are in effect, turn left from the Ohlone Trail onto the Bay Laurel Trail and continue for 0.1 mile. Then turn left on the Meadowlark Trail and follow the directions below. This loop route is 2.5 miles long and has 300 feet of elevation gain.)

At 1 mile, head right and downhill on the fragrant and aptly named Bay Laurel Trail, where you'll see bay laurels, oaks, toyons, and lots of poison oak. At 1.2 miles, turn right on the paved Woodland Star Trail, then take a quick jog left through a first seasonal closure gate onto a singletrack dirt trail (also the Woodland Star Trail).

In 0.4 mile, reach another seasonal closure gate, and just after this, at 1.6 miles, turn left on the Meadowlark Trail. At this junction, there is a large and lovely oak with a bench for taking in the views. Here you start getting views of the Stanford Dish (Hike 22), the Bay, Mission Peak, Mount Allison with its many towers, and Monument Peak with a few towers on it. You'll also see fancy homes in the nearby hills.

Stay on the Meadowlark Trail until 2.4 miles, passing four connections with the Bowl Loop and finally turning left toward the vista point. Here, enjoy a quick 0.2-mile roundtrip detour to the viewpoint, which has another impressive oak tree with a bench underneath it and views all the way to San Francisco and Marin's Mount Tamalpais. After this, the route trends downhill the rest of the way.

Once back at the Meadowlark Trail, turn left, and after a short distance, pass through a seasonal closure gate. Continue almost half a mile (until 2.9 miles total), taking in more sweeping views. At the end of this stretch, pass through a final seasonal closure gate, which ends in a T. Turn right to stay on the Meadowlark Trail, and then turn left after a few hundred feet (3.2 miles total) to continue on the Meadowlark Trail. Stay on the

Meadowlark Trail for a final 0.3 mile until you reach the de Anza Trail, where you turn right.

At 3.2 miles, stay on the de Anza Trail for 0.4 mile, passing the Arastradero Creek Trail, Arastradero Lake, and the Paseo del Roble Trail on your right. At 3.6 miles, reach a junction with the Meadowlark Trail where you were earlier on this hike. Return the way you came, staying on the de Anza Trail to Arastradero Road, then crossing the street to return to the parking lot.

GO FARTHER

Add the 1.5-mile Redtail Loop Trail to the beginning or end of your hike. This trail starts right from the parking lot. Gain some elevation while taking in eastward views of Stanford, Palo Alto, and the Bay.

22 Stanford Dish

DISTANCE: 3.6 miles
ELEVATION GAIN: 550 feet
HIGH POINT: 810 feet
DIFFICULTY: Moderate
TIME: 1 hour and 15 minutes
FITNESS: Hikers, fit walkers, runners
FAMILY-FRIENDLY: Yes, but some sections may be too steep for small children, some walkers, or those walking with strollers.
DOG-FRIENDLY: No
AMENITIES: Restroom, accessible trails (some steep sections may be difficult for manual wheelchair users)
CONTACT: Stanford University (SRI International owns the Dish itself)
BEFORE YOU GO: The park has different opening hours each month. Check the Stanford Dish Area website for hours.
GPS: 37° 24' 36.5976" N, 122° 9' 40.0212" W

The best time to visit the Dish is in springtime when the grass is green and the wildflowers are out. (Photo: Yasaman Mohsenin)

GETTING THERE

Map to: Stanford Dish Hiking Trailhead, Stanford. **Public Transit:** Take Stanford Marguerite Shuttle line Y to the Campus Drive at Wilbur Field stop (1.1 miles from hike start) or Line C to the Bowdoin Street at Pine Hill Court stop (0.8 mile from hike start). **Parking:** Parking can be a challenge! Limited free parking is available along Stanford Avenue. Arrive early or be prepared to wait for a spot.

The Dish is a Peninsula classic. It's not too long but still hilly, so you'll get a workout and nice Peninsula and Bay views. The route is paved, so there's no worrying about uneven terrain. And you'll hike this loop clockwise so that you'll do most of the climbing at the start. I recommend this route in

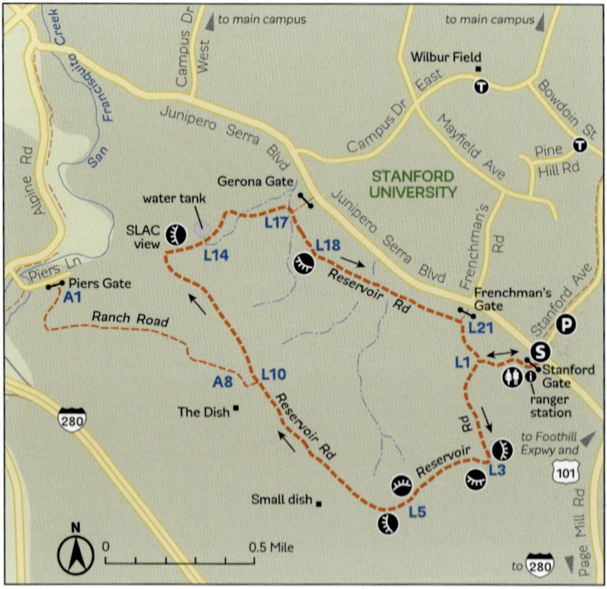

spring when the grass surrounding the trail is green and the weather's not too hot.

Of course, the main sight on this route is the Stanford University radio telescope—a satellite dish—commonly called "the Dish." It was built in 1961 by SRI International (formerly Stanford Research Institute). Stanford's website says the Dish was designed to send signals through the Earth's ionosphere, but SRI engineer Stephen Muther shared on the KQED *Bay Curious* podcast that the Dish was built to collect intelligence on Russia after the launch of Sputnik 1. It delivered on its mission and was able to intercept Soviet signals as they bounced off the moon.

GET MOVING

The Dish is a straightforward route. If you don't need directions, just follow the map! For those who want more information, I've noted some of the many trail markers and points of interest below.

Start at the intersection of Junipero Serra Boulevard and Stanford Avenue, where you'll find a ranger station and the only restroom on this route. Pick up the paved trail, where you head uphill for about a quarter mile. At the L1 trail marker continue straight and uphill. (You'll be back at this junction at the end of the hike.)

Pass through a small cluster of oaks (your only shade on this route), and at 0.3 mile, you'll see a turnoff to your right, the first of many off-limits sections just to the side of the trail. As you continue climbing, turn around to see the Bay, Mount Diablo, and Mount Hamilton.

At 0.6 mile (L3), the trail bends right, and you get your first view of one of two satellite dishes on this trail. On your left, you can see Mount Umunhum. If you turn around, you can see Stanford's Hoover Tower. At 0.8 mile, just after marker L5, you reach the highest elevation on this hike. On a clear day, you can see San Francisco and Mount Tamalpais off to your right in the distance.

You reach a smaller satellite dish 0.2 mile after this. Then, at 1.6 miles, you arrive at the larger 150-foot diameter satellite dish that is this route's namesake. As you pass the Dish, you start to see and hear car noise from Interstate 280 off to the left.

As you pass marker L10, you can extend the hike by up to 2.2 miles (see Go Farther), and at marker L14, you'll pass a reservoir. Look behind you to see the buildings of the Stanford Linear Accelerator Center (SLAC), a laboratory devoted to experimental and theoretical research in elementary particle physics. At 2.7 miles, when you reach marker L17, head right and uphill. As you get to the top of a slight incline at marker L18, you'll get a nice view of the Dish again. You're now on a flat section that will take you back to marker L1, the first junction you encountered on this trail. At L2, head downhill and left about a quarter mile back to the start.

GO FARTHER

Extend your hike by up to 2.2 miles by hiking down to the Piers Gate. To do this, walk up to the Dish and pick up Ranch Road, where you'll find trail markers A8 to A1. When you arrive at the Piers Gate exit, turn around and head back to the Dish.

23 Foothills Nature Preserve

DISTANCE: 3.8 miles
ELEVATION GAIN: 820 feet
HIGH POINT: 1,000 feet
DIFFICULTY: Moderate
TIME: 2 hours
FITNESS: Hikers, walkers, runners. The elevation gain may be too much for some walkers. Stroll the paved road between Foothills Nature Interpretive Center and Boronda Lake for a flat alternative.
FAMILY-FRIENDLY: See above.
DOG-FRIENDLY: Dogs allowed on leash on weekdays. No dogs allowed on weekends.
AMENITIES: Restrooms, benches, picnic areas, pay phones, water refill station at the interpretive center and park entrance
CONTACT: City of Palo Alto
BEFORE YOU GO: There are driving roads throughout the park. Watch out for cars.
GPS: 37° 21' 47.8152" N, 122° 11' 9.7908" W

GETTING THERE

Map to: Foothills Park Nature Interpretive Center, 3300 Page Mill Road, Palo Alto. **Parking:** Park next to the Foothills Nature Preserve Interpretive Center. Passenger cars pay a small fee for entry. Additional parking is available in the Orchard Glen and Oak Grove parking areas.

Foothills Nature Preserve features scrub habitats, grasslands, and woodlands, and I see deer every time I visit.

An Ohlone hunting ground for 3,000 years, today Foothills Nature Preserve comprises 1,400 acres and 15 miles of hiking trails. Dr. Russel V. A. Lee, a founder of Palo Alto Medical Clinic (later part of the Palo Alto Medical Foundation), sold this land to Palo Alto in 1958 on the condition that the city preserve it as open space. The park was dedicated in 1965, and in 1969, Palo Alto began limiting access to residents and their guests. People fought to make this land public for decades, and finally a 2020 lawsuit forced the city to open the park to all.

On this moderate route with some steep ascents, you'll explore a variety of park scenery, including chaparral,

woodlands, grasslands, a lake, and a viewpoint over the Peninsula. Animals thrive here, so it's not uncommon to see deer or hear turkeys warbling while you hike.

GET MOVING

Start the hike at the Foothills Nature Preserve Interpretive Center. Pick up the Chamise Trail on your left about 450 feet east of the center. You'll be on this trail until 0.6 mile. Halfway through this stretch, you'll reach a turnoff for the Arbolejo Overlook. Explore the overlook if you'd like a rest from this first climb. There is a bench at the end of the overlook and some views, but I personally think the views are better later on at Vista Hill. (This optional detour is not included in the selected route mileage.)

About 0.2 mile later, arrive at a sign for Vista Hill in 0.1 mile. Continue to a road and cross it. Then climb a narrow dirt path to the top of Vista Hill. The path arrives at a parking area with a pedestrian path around the overlook. From Vista Hill, look for the Dish (Hike 22), Stanford's Hoover Tower, and Moffett Field. On clear days, you can also see San Francisco. Return to the junction with the sign for Vista Hill in 0.1 mile.

This time, head left and downhill to explore a new part of the Chamise Trail featuring large grassy expanses. When you reach a road at 1.1 miles, cross it, head left, and then quickly pick up a trail on your right that lines Boronda Lake. There are two paths you can choose from, and you can take either, as they eventually merge.

Continue on the path for 0.4 mile to the park entrance, with an optional visit, via bridge, to teeny tiny Sunfish Island halfway along your way. Once at the park entrance, you'll find restrooms, informational signage, water, and trash cans. Next to the informational signage, pick up the Toyon Trail on your right, a 1-mile self-guided nature trail with twenty-five numbered points of interest. As you climb this shaded singletrack trail, you'll see ferns, miner's lettuce, bay laurels, and of course toyons! Pass the Woodrat Trail at 1.8 miles, then look right at interpretive markers 7 and 8 to see the Dish again.

In 0.3 mile after the Woodrat Trail junction, you've reached this route's highest elevation. Head downhill, and just after marker 21, use the middle path when you see three trails in front of you at 2.4 miles.

When the Toyon Trail ends 0.2 mile later, use a bridge to cross Buckeye Creek. Head right on a fire road, then turn left on the Steep Hollow Trail at 2.7 miles. Oaks, bay laurels, ferns, and other low-lying plants surround this shaded singletrack trail. At 3 miles total, take a sharp right on the Sunrise Trail. Wind uphill on this narrow trail through more toyons and scrub plants. On this stretch, look for Mount Diablo on the right. At 3.3 miles, stay right at a trail marker to pick up the Los Trancos Trail for half a mile.

Bay laurels, ferns, and poison oak surround you. On some parts of this downhill section, you can see Mount Diablo and Boronda Lake. On other parts, you'll duck into tree cover. At the end of the Los Trancos Trail, use the Los Trancos Bridge to cross Buckeye Creek again. You'll see the Foothills Nature Preserve Interpretive Center in front of you.

GO FARTHER

To take a longer hike, start on the Coyote Trail. Be sure to spend some time in the Foothills Nature Preserve Interpretive Center, which was once Russel V. A. Lee's barn and stable. The Center features photos of wildflowers that grow in the park as well as taxidermied birds and mammals that once lived here.

24 Baylands Nature Preserve

DISTANCE: 5.5 miles
ELEVATION GAIN: 0 feet
HIGH POINT: 0 feet
DIFFICULTY: Easy
TIME: 2 hours and 15 minutes
FITNESS: Hikers, walkers, runners
FAMILY-FRIENDLY: These flat trails are great for families. You can turn around at any time to make this hike as short or long as you like.
DOG-FRIENDLY: Yes, on leash
AMENITIES: Restrooms, water, benches
CONTACT: City of Palo Alto
BEFORE YOU GO: This trail is accessible for wheelchair users.
GPS: 37° 24' 17.496" N, 122° 6' 40.752" W

GETTING THERE

Map to: Terminal Boulevard and San Antonio Road, Mountain View. **Public Transit:** Take MVgo buses C or D to the Marine at Casey stop (weekday commute hours) or the VTA ACE Orange shuttle to the San Antonio and Casey stop. This is one block from the hike start. **Parking:** Free street parking is available near Terminal Boulevard and San Antonio Road.

The 1,940 acres of Baylands Nature Preserve reach from East Palo Alto to Mountain View, comprising one of the

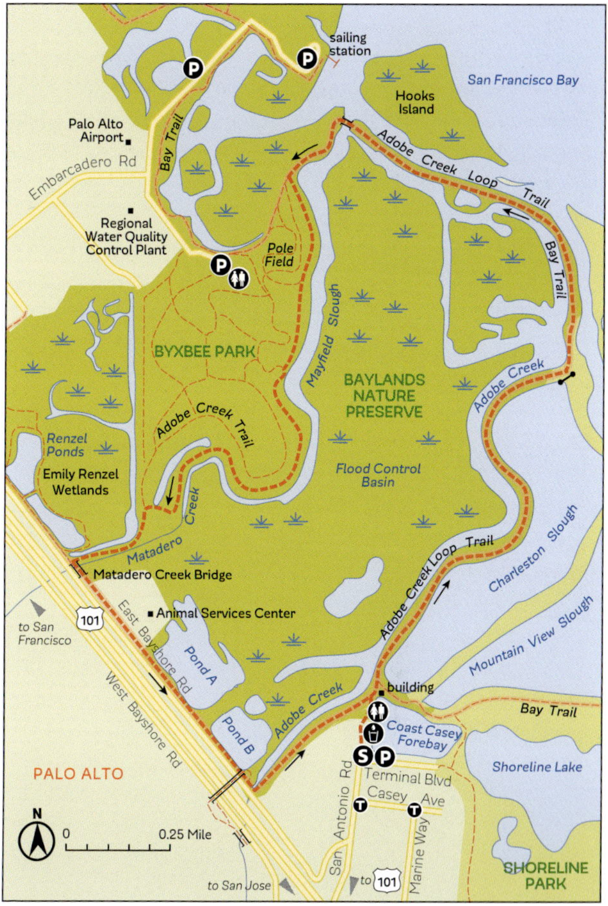

largest spans of contiguous marshland in the Bay Area. This area also includes some of the last remaining salt marsh and mudflat habitats on the West Coast, making it a prime spot for bird-watching. Countless birds call this area home, including the endangered California clapper rail and Ridgway's rail, and many others fly through here as a stop on the Pacific Flyway.

Of course, this park is great for hikers, too. Hikers can enjoy 15 miles of flat waterside trails, and the selected route is an easy loop around Adobe Creek. The last part of the route runs along East Bayshore Road and is close to traffic noise from US 101. However, the rest of the route is quite peaceful, so enjoy it!

GET MOVING

From Terminal Boulevard and San Antonio Road, look for a paved trail behind a metal gate. A green sign reading "Shoreline at Mountain View" greets you. Just after this, you'll reach the only restroom on the route.

Walk 0.2 mile to a junction marked by a small concrete brick building. Stay straight here to pick up the Adobe Creek Loop Trail. The path soon turns to gravel, and you're in a wide marshy area. To your right, you can see the twin tented towers of Shoreline Amphitheatre in the distance. Continue along a narrow strip of land with Adobe Creek on your left and Charleston Slough on your right.

At 1.3 miles, head left at a trail marker that says "1.5 mi to Byxbee Park Lot." The Bay is now on your right, and

Baylands Nature Preserve is along the Pacific Flyway. (Photo: Dan Luscher)

you can see the Dumbarton Bridge in the distance. There are powerlines alongside the trail, and you may also see airplanes flying to and from Palo Alto Airport. Along with grasses and cord grasses, California sagebrush and fennel now line the trail.

At 2.3 miles, take a bridge (really a tide gate) across Mayfield Slough. Then, at 2.5 miles, reach a junction with three options. Stay left along the water, following a trail sign that says "1.7 miles to Renzel Wetlands." (Alternatively, you can take the right trail to head into Byxbee Park; see Go Farther.)

At the start of this stretch, you'll encounter Byxbee Park's *Pole Field*, an installation by environmental artists Peter Richards and Michael Oppenheimer. These artists, along with landscape architects Hargreaves Associates, helped create Byxbee Park in 1990 and 1991. The installation was designed for birds to perch on, and while it started out uniform, some of the poles no longer stand straight due to the ground settling in this former landfill.

At 3.9 miles, arrive at a T and turn left. You'll encounter some larger trees as you enter the Emily Renzel Wetlands. Continue a quarter mile to reach East Bayshore Road. Use the Matadero Creek Bridge to turn left and walk along a paved bike path next to a busy, unscenic road for three-quarters of a mile. At the end of this stretch, cross a bridge after an overpass and look for a path on your left that leads back into Baylands. There is a sign here for Mountain View Shoreline Park. (If you pass 3803 East Bayshore Road, you've gone too far.)

Pick up a multiuse trail where you see a trail marker for the Adobe Creek Loop Trail. Stay on this path until 5.3 miles total to arrive at the concrete brick building you saw at the start of the hike. Turn right and walk 0.2 mile back to the start.

GO FARTHER

Explore Byxbee Park to see more art installations or for an extra restroom on the route.

25 Sunnyvale Bay Trail

DISTANCE:	5 miles
ELEVATION GAIN:	10 feet
HIGH POINT:	10 feet
DIFFICULTY:	Easy
TIME:	2 hours
FITNESS:	Hikers, walkers, runners
FAMILY-FRIENDLY:	Yes
DOG-FRIENDLY:	Yes, on leash, but don't confuse this route with neighboring Sunnyvale Baylands Park, where dogs are prohibited.
AMENITIES:	Restroom, benches
CONTACT:	San Francisco Bay Trail
GPS:	37° 25' 3.4644" N, 122° 1' 8.148" W

GETTING THERE

Map to: 293-327 W Caribbean Drive, Sunnyvale. **Public Transit:** The VTA Orange Line Borregas stop is 0.4 mile from the hike start. **Parking:** Free street parking is available along West Caribbean Drive and Caribbean Drive between Mathilda and Borregas Avenues.

Unlike other hikes in this book, this route doesn't belong to a particular park. Instead, it's part of Guadalupe Slough. This was once the mouth of the Guadalupe River (which has since been rerouted to Alviso Slough), and now several local creeks flow here. This is also part of the larger San Francisco Bay Trail, which will one day be a 500-mile contiguous trail around the Bay.

The trails are located behind the Sunnyvale Water Pollution Control Plant (WPCP). While that might not sounN too appealing, after 0.2 mile, the scenery opens up and the crowds thin out. As you complete a 5-mile loop around the Sunnyvale WPCP West Pond, you'll get views of Diablo Range mountains, Moffett Field, and of course the Bay. This

is a great spot for bird-watching but not for swimming. While the water looks nice, remember that it's part of a sewage treatment pond.

GET MOVING

From W. Caribbean Drive, pick up the wide gravel Bay Trail about halfway between North Mathilda and Borregas Avenues. After 0.1 mile, continue straight (or right to visit the only restroom on the route). There's a stairway to your left that you can climb later (see Go Farther).

At 0.2 mile, stay straight as a path branches off to the left. Just after this, follow the trail as it bends right. At 0.6 mile, bear right to head toward the Federal Aviation Administration (FAA) radar tower (or head left and go around a gate to cut 0.7 mile off the total route mileage; see Make It Shorter). Speaking of

The Sunnyvale Bay Trail is a flat multi-use trail with pleasant water and mountain views.

the FAA, you're on the flight path for San Jose Airport, and you'll likely see planes overhead as you hike.

At 0.7 mile, walk around a gate to continue on the trail. Take in the view of Mission Peak ahead of you, Mount Allison with multiple towers to the right of Mission Peak, and Monument Peak with a few towers to the right of Mount Allison.

Continue 0.6 mile, following the trail as it bends left and away from the mountains at marker 11. Then stay straight in 350 feet at marker 12. On this stretch, look for Mount Tamalpais in the distance to the north. After half a mile, continue straight at marker 16.

At 2.5 miles, reach marker 21 as the trail bends to the left. You are now facing Moffett Field. Then, at 3.1 miles, you can take the trail on your left or continue along the trail you're on, which bends left at marker 25 just ahead. These two trails run parallel for the next section of the route. From either trail, you will be facing Mount Hamilton. After a mile, the trail bends left, and at 4.3 miles, make a sharp right and return the way you came. (If you took the inner trail, you'll head a little farther before you can make two right turns to return to the start.)

GO FARTHER

Climb the stairway you passed at the end of this hike for a little elevation (about 65 feet) that'll give you an aerial view of the route you just completed.

MAKE IT SHORTER

For a 4.3-mile route, head left at the FAA radar tower 0.6 mile into the hike. This will take you to marker 16, where you can continue to follow the selected route.

26 Rancho San Antonio

DISTANCE: 5.4 miles
ELEVATION GAIN: 900 feet
HIGH POINT: 940 feet
DIFFICULTY: Moderate
TIME: 2 hours and 30 minutes
FITNESS: Hikers, walkers, runners
FAMILY-FRIENDLY: Yes, walkers and families can head to Deer Hollow Farm and back on accessible trails.
DOG-FRIENDLY: No
AMENITIES: Restrooms, water, benches, picnic areas, viewpoint, accessible trails
CONTACT: Midpeninsula Regional Open Space District
GPS: 37° 19' 49.44" N, 122° 5' 7.4904" W

GETTING THERE

Map to: Rancho San Antonio County Park and Open Space Preserve, parking lot 1. **Public Transit:** VTA Route 51 stops at Foothill Boulevard and Starling Drive, a 1.4-mile walk from the hike start. **Parking:** Free parking. Even with over three hundred parking spaces, finding a free spot on weekends can still be tricky. Arrive early or mid-afternoon after the morning hiking rush.

Rancho San Antonio's parking situation will make you feel like everyone in the Bay Area had the same idea at the same time. Even with six lots near the main entrance, spots are often sparse or unavailable on weekends. Once you secure a spot, you'll be contending with crowds for the first mile of your hike. However, as you venture farther, the crowds thin out and you'll see why everyone came here in the first place. The area features a whopping 25 miles of trails with varied scenery just a quick drive from several Peninsula cities.

This route links several of the best trails into a loop that highlights the charming Deer Hollow Farm, a spectacular view over Silicon Valley, the singletrack Wildcat Loop Trail, and the Stephen E. Abbors Trail, which has some tree cover and views from San Jose to Marin's Mount Tamalpais.

GET MOVING

This route starts in parking lot 1 and passes by parking lot 6. Wherever you park, just head to either of these lots. The mileage for this write-up starts from parking lot 1.

Head to the back of the parking lot 1 and turn right on the South Meadow Trail, a wide, flat dirt trail. When you reach lot 6 after 0.2 mile, turn left and walk through a gate onto the paved Rancho San Antonio Service Road. After 425 feet, take your first right off the road onto a narrower paved road (ignoring two turnoffs on the left before this). Quickly cross a paved bike path (look for a bridge on your right) and

Rancho San Antonio's crowds diminish once you pass Deer Hollow Farm, and you may even have some of the trails to yourself.

continue to a gravel path, following a sign for the Permanente Creek Trail.

At 0.5 mile, follow the trail as it branches left. Walk through an area lined with a fence on both sides and pass a paved trail. Then, at a large "Rancho San Antonio" sign, stay straight to pick up the Lower Meadow Trail toward Deer Hollow Farm. At 0.8 mile, cross a crosswalk and choose between a dirt pedestrian-only trail and a paved bike-friendly trail. Either way, you'll end up at a multitrail junction at 1.1 miles. Here, continue on the paved or dirt trail toward Deer Hollow Farm. At 1.2 miles, the paths merge and you cross over a bridge. Then, at 1.3 miles, you reach Deer Hollow Farm, where you'll see historic buildings, an organic garden, and animals! You can pet the resident cats and get close-up views of cows, sheep, goats, pigs, and chickens. Spend as much time at the farm as you like and then rejoin the trail. At a covered picnic area, pass through a gate, then turn left toward the Wildcat Loop Trail.

You'll quickly come upon some restrooms. Just after the restrooms, the trail splits. Stay right on the wide dirt Wildcat Loop Trail. Then take a right on the High Meadow Trail at 1.5 miles. Head up a series of switchbacks through shade and clearings, where you'll start to take in views of the Peninsula and the Diablo Range.

At 2.4 miles, turn left at a five-way junction to explore a vista point a few hundred feet ahead. Here you get expansive Peninsula views along with views of Diablo Range mountains, including Mission Peak, Monument Peak, and Mount Allison. You can see Shoreline Amphitheatre, Moffett Field, Apple's Infinite Loop, Levi's Stadium, and downtown San Jose.

Return to the junction you took to the vista point and turn left on the Wildcat Loop Trail at 2.4 miles. Enjoy a pleasant 0.6-mile mostly downhill section lined with chaparral as well as toyons, bay laurels, and oaks. At 3 miles, turn left and head over a bridge. When you reach a cluster of trees, turn right toward the Stephen E. Abbors Trail. In another 0.1 mile when you reach a T, turn left to pick up the Stephen E. Abbors Trail in the direction of "County Park". You'll be on this trail for 1.6 miles, the first 0.7 mile of which is uphill. You'll see many electrical towers along this trail—it was a PG&E service road called the PG&E Trail until 2018. In addition to the electrical towers, you'll also get scenic views of the Santa Clara Valley and all the way north to Mount Tamalpais.

At 4.9 miles, at a five-way junction near a water tank, head right on the Coyote Trail. You'll start in a wooded canyon and end with views of nearby homes and grasslands dotted with oak trees. After half a mile, stay straight to cross a bridge to parking lot 1.

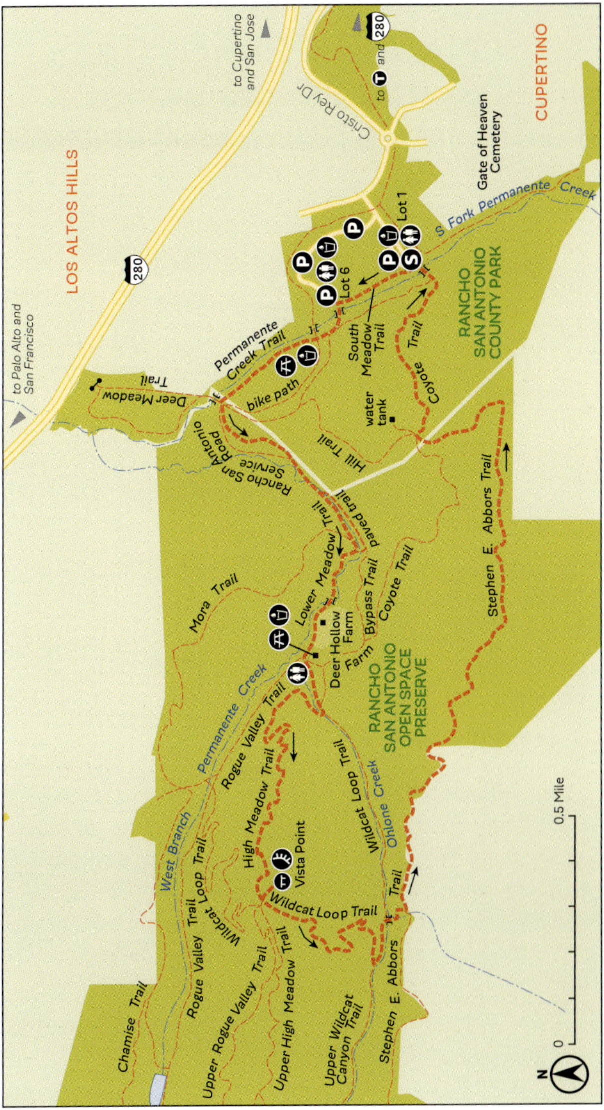
LOS ALTOS HILLS
CUPERTINO
to Palo Alto and San Francisco
to Cupertino and San Jose
280
to and 280
Cristo Rey Dr
Gate of Heaven Cemetery
S Fork Permanente Creek
Lot 1
Lot 6
South Meadow Trail
Permanente Creek Trail
bike path
Deer Meadow Trail
Coyote Trail
water tank
Hill Trail
RANCHO SAN ANTONIO COUNTY PARK
Rancho San Antonio Service Road
paved trail
Lower Meadow Trail
Bypass Trail
Mora Trail
Deer Hollow Farm
Farm
Stephen E. Abbors Trail
RANCHO SAN ANTONIO OPEN SPACE PRESERVE
Permanente Creek
Rogue Valley Trail
High Meadow Trail
Wildcat Loop Trail
Ohlone Creek
Vista Point
Wildcat Loop Trail
West Branch
Wildcat Loop Trail
Rogue Valley Trail
Chamise Trail
Upper Rogue Valley Trail
Upper High Meadow Trail
Upper Wildcat Canyon Trail
Stephen E. Abbors Trail
0.5 Mile
0
N

27 Picchetti Ranch Open Space Preserve

DISTANCE: 4.2 miles
ELEVATION GAIN: 750 feet
HIGH POINT: 990 feet
DIFFICULTY: Easy to moderate
TIME: 1 hour and 45 minutes
FITNESS: Hikers, walkers
FAMILY-FRIENDLY: Yes, this route is great for a hike and a picnic. You may turn around any time to shorten the route.
DOG-FRIENDLY: No
AMENITIES: Restrooms, water, picnic area, winery
CONTACT: Midpeninsula Regional Open Space District
BEFORE YOU GO: Bring a picnic lunch; no food sold on site.
GPS: 37° 17' 41.5788" N, 122° 5' 28.4244" W

GETTING THERE

Map to: Picchetti Ranch Open Space Preserve, 13100 Montebello Road. **Parking:** Free parking with eighty standard spaces and two ADA spaces.

Picchetti Ranch Open Space Preserve is a perfect day trip. After you hike this route on trails lined with oaks, toyons, and fragrant bay laurels, you can relax with a picnic or wine tasting.

Secundo and Vincenzo Picchetti bought 160 acres here in 1872 and named the ridge they planted on "Montebello." The Picchetti family produced wine here for seventy-two years between the 1890s and the 1960s. Then, in 1976, the Midpeninsula Regional Open Space District bought the land. Sunrise Winery operated here between 1982 and 1997. Since then, Leslie Pantling and her family have been producing wine here under the Picchetti name. They produce around 10,000 cases annually, and you can purchase the wine only on site.

Whether or not you're imbibing, pop into the tasting room, which was completed in 1896. Also, keep an eye out for peacocks, which have roamed the property since the Picchettis brought them here in the 1890s.

GET MOVING

Start this route behind the historical brick Picchetti Winery building. Walk through a gate to pick up the Zinfandel Trail, a wide dirt trail where you'll find restrooms immediately off to your left. Head uphill to see Mission Peak, Mount Allison, and

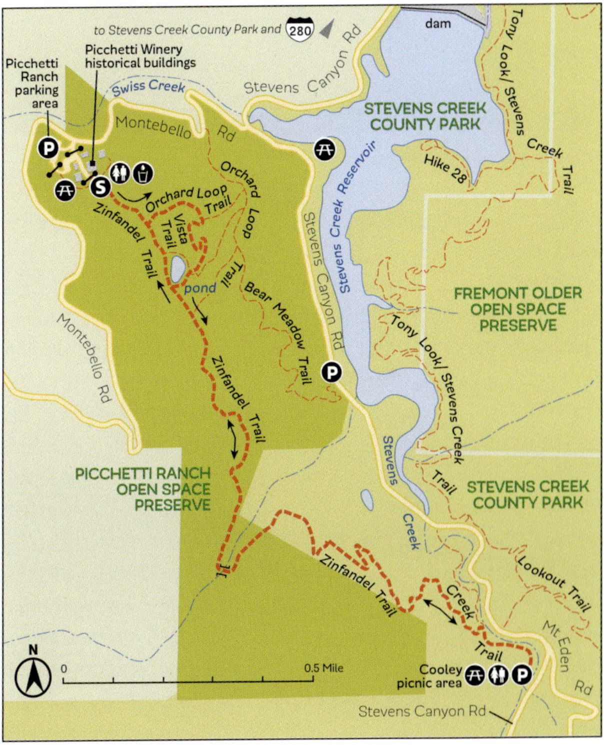

A young hiker spots Stevens Creek Reservoir from the Zinfandel Trail.

Monument Peak off to your left. The Stevens Creek Quarry is visible behind you.

After 0.2 mile, turn left to pick up the Orchard Loop Trail, where you continue uphill. Take the next right on the Vista Trail, a lovely trail shaded with oak trees. You soon turn left and head downhill, following a sign for the Vista Trail and the pond. At 0.5 mile total, continue straight at an intersection to reach the pond (which can be completely dry depending on the season). Continue a bit further to reach the Zinfandel Trail, where you turn left.

At 0.6 mile, stay straight on the Zinfandel Trail at its junction with the Orchard Loop Trail. Continue on this trail for 1.6 more miles (until 2.2 miles total). The singletrack trail winds around a canyon, offering views of Stevens Creek Reservoir and the surrounding mountains. It then descends over 300 feet into an oak, toyon, and bay laurel forest—elevation you'll need to regain on your return trip. If you want to keep the elevation gain to the minimum on this route, see Make It Shorter.

At 1.9 mile, look out for a T with another trail. Head left and then take a quick jog right to continue on the Zinfandel Trail. At 2.1 mile, reach a junction with the Creek Trail, where you continue straight to hike a final 0.1 mile to the Cooley picnic area, which has picnic tables, trash cans, water, and restrooms. For the return trip, take the Zinfandel Trail 2 miles back to the start.

GO FARTHER

Pack a picnic lunch, do a wine tasting, or pick up a bottle of wine at Picchetti Winery.

MAKE IT SHORTER

If you're looking to minimize the elevation gain on this hike, do the 2.1-mile version of this route instead, which has only 300 feet of elevation gain. Follow the start of the route as written above. When you reach a wood bridge at 1.2 miles, turn around and return 1 mile on the Zinfandel Trail back to the start.

28 Stevens Creek County Park

DISTANCE:	2.9 miles
ELEVATION GAIN:	270 feet
HIGH POINT:	550 feet
DIFFICULTY:	Easy
TIME:	1 hour and 30 minutes
FITNESS:	Hikers, walkers, runners
FAMILY-FRIENDLY:	Yes
DOG-FRIENDLY:	Yes, on leash
AMENITIES:	Restrooms, benches, picnic areas
CONTACT:	Santa Clara County Parks
BEFORE YOU GO:	Make sure to bring a credit card to pay for parking.
GPS:	37° 18' 22.5756" N, 122° 4' 29.1756" W

Walking along 82-acre reservoir is one of the highlights of this route in Stevens Creek County Park.

GETTING THERE

Map to: Stevens Creek County Park, 11401 Stevens Canyon Road. **Parking:** Pay a small fee for parking using the kiosk in the Chestnut parking area. There are dozens of standard spaces and three ADA spaces. Villa Maria picnic area has parking if the Chestnut lot is full.

The 1,063-acre Stevens Creek County Park features 9 miles of trails. The park is named for Captain Elisha Stevens (also spelled Elijah Stephens), who in 1844 led the first successful wagon train over the Sierra Nevada mountains.

The featured route gives you a balance of forested and exposed trails, plus a close-up of the dam and the 87-acre Stevens Creek Reservoir. While this route is rated easy, there are a few short, steep ascents and descents to be aware of. This is a popular destination, and the Tony Look/Stevens Creek Trail can be busy on weekends. Despite all the people, I've still seen deer here every time I've visited. While you'll encounter fewer people on the Rim Trail, it can be noisier due to its proximity to Stevens Canyon Road. Do this route

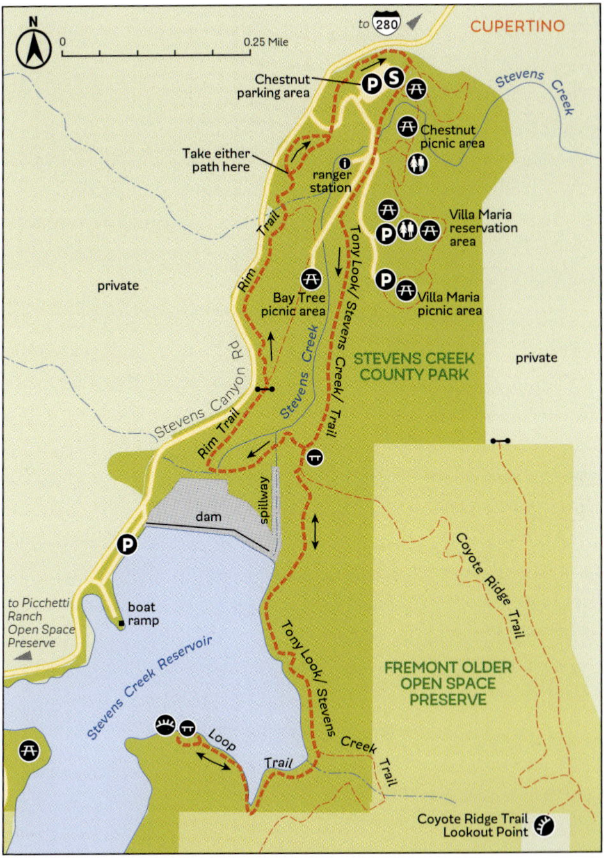

if you're in the mood for a low-key nature stroll. This is also one of the few area parks that welcomes dogs, so bring your favorite pup!

GET MOVING

Start the hike in the Chestnut parking area. Take a dirt trail starting at the lot (near the striped crosswalk) and follow it to a paved road where you turn left (be careful to watch for cars). Bear right following a sign for the Park Office. Then, 0.1 mile later, turn off the paved road and head onto a wide fire trail known as the Tony Look/Stevens Creek Trail.

This trail runs along Stevens Creek and is lined with oaks, bay laurels, and toyons as well as poison oak. At 0.5 mile, reach an open area with a bench. There is a junction here with the Rim Trail. You'll be back here later, but for now, continue on the Tony Look/Stevens Creek Trail.

When you reach a junction after 150 feet, head right and uphill. The trail quickly flattens, and you'll begin walking along the Stevens Creek Reservoir. At 0.9 mile, stay straight to pick up the Loop Trail. Continue another 0.4 mile to complete a loop around a lookout with a bench where you can take in views of the reservoir. Return the way you came, heading 0.7 mile back to the junction with the Rim Trail.

At this junction, head left and downhill. The trail quickly flattens out, and you'll be walking behind the dam for 0.2 mile. The trail is more exposed here and is lined by scrub plants. At 2.3 miles, reach a gate at Stevens Canyon Road. Stay to the right of the gate to stay on the Rim Trail. Soon after this, the trail splits. Stay left on the dirt Rim Trail (do not take the paved trail).

At 2.5 miles, leave this wider trail and turn left at an easy-to-miss Rim Trail sign. Then, in 0.1 mile, reach a T where you can make a left or right. Both sides of the trail converge after a few hundred feet. Almost immediately after this, cross a road (looking carefully for cars) and continue on the Rim Trail. Here you'll be walking above the Chestnut parking area and Stevens Canyon Road. The trail drops you back in the parking area after 0.2 mile.

GO FARTHER

For a hike in this park with more elevation, climb up the Coyote Ridge Trail or climb Maisie's Peak and Nob Hill in neighboring Fremont Older Open Space Preserve (Hike 29).

29 Fremont Older Open Space Preserve

DISTANCE:	4.5 miles
ELEVATION GAIN:	840 feet
HIGH POINT:	1,181 feet
DIFFICULTY:	Moderate
TIME:	2 hours and 15 minutes
FITNESS:	Hikers, runners
FAMILY-FRIENDLY:	Families and walkers may enjoy a hike to Hunter's Point (see Make It Shorter).
DOG-FRIENDLY:	Yes
AMENITIES:	Restroom at the start of the hike, bench on top of Nob Hill
CONTACT:	Midpeninsula Regional Open Space District
BEFORE YOU GO:	This hike is largely exposed and can be hot in summer. If you can, hike in another season.
GPS:	37° 17' 9.4632" N, 122° 3' 18.7488" W

GETTING THERE

Map to: Prospect parking area, Prospect Road, Saratoga. **Parking:** The Prospect parking area has twenty standard spaces and one ADA space. The lot can fill up quickly on weekends, so arrive early or come after the morning rush.

Fremont Older (1856–1935) was a local newspaper editor who, along with his wife Cora, owned part of this land for sixty years and lived in a home they called "Woodhills." Nearby, David and Sophia Garrod moved to the United States from England in 1892 and established a farm here in 1893. Descendants of this family still own and operate Garrod Farms, which includes stables and an estate winery.

On this route, you'll hike through grasslands, chaparral, and oak woodlands to reach two scenic viewpoints: Maisie's Peak and Nob Hill. Maisie's Peak, the highest point in the preserve, is named for Maisie Garrod, one of David and Sophia's three children. While you hike, look down for horse poop, look out for bikers, and look up to catch expansive Santa Clara Valley panoramas from the two viewpoints.

GET MOVING

From the parking lot, pick up the paved road (watch out for cars). After 0.1 mile, turn right on the Creekside Trail, a shaded singletrack trail heading steeply uphill. At 0.3 mile, turn right and head toward Hunter's Point, Regnart Road, and Stevens Creek County Park. The historic former Older residence is just off this junction. It's currently a private residence, so please don't disturb the occupants.

You're now on a fire road heading uphill through grasslands dotted with oak trees. After 0.1 mile, pass the Cora Older Trail on your right. At the next junction, turn left away from the Seven Springs Loop Trail, and in a few hundred feet turn left to pick up the Hayfield Trail. Continue here for half a mile, passing a turnoff for the Toyon Trail along the way. The trail is lined with scrub oaks, coyote brush, California sagebrush, poison oak, yarrow, and the occasional oak tree. Look for views of Mount Umunhum and Mount Hamilton.

The Hayfield Trail dead-ends into the Coyote Ridge Trail at 1.1 mile. Turn left here toward Garrod Farms and continue for 0.3 mile, passing junctions for the Fern Trail on the right and the Bay View Trail on the left. When you reach a junction with the Vista Loop Trail on the right, pass it and turn left toward Maisie's Peak (elevation 1,181 feet) a short distance later. This roundtrip trail takes you to the highest point in the park in a few hundred feet.

Return to and continue on the Coyote Ridge Trail another 0.4 mile to a five-way junction, ignoring a junction with the Vista Loop Trail halfway through this stretch. On your right at this large junction, you see the vineyards at Garrod Farms. Continue straight and slightly uphill, passing the sign for the farm on your right. The trail curves to the left and then to the

This route in Fremont Older visits two scenic viewpoints: Maisie's Peak and Nob Hill (pictured).

right. At 2.3 miles, turn right to complete a 0.2-mile roundtrip exploration of Nob Hill (elevation 1,138 feet). At the summit, a bench is dedicated to the Cooper and Garrod families. (Louise Garrod, David and Sophia's grandchild, met George

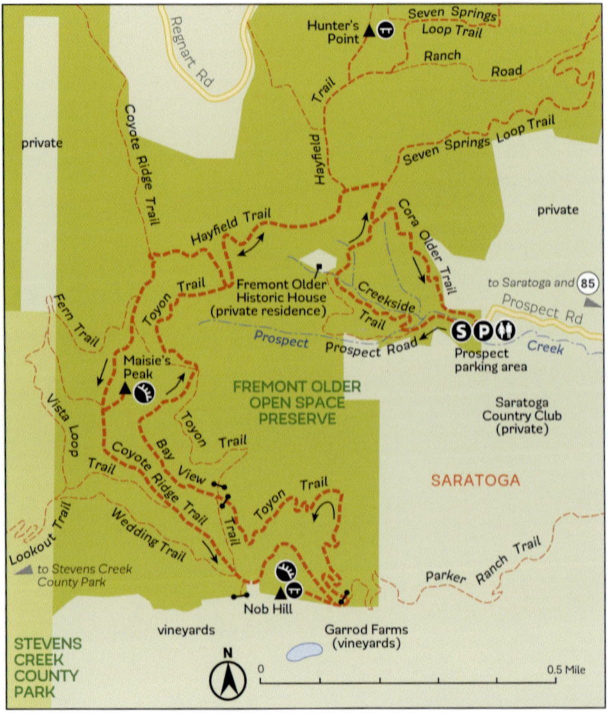

Cooper at the University of California, Berkeley. The couple married and had four children.)

Descend the hill and continue straight. After 150 feet, turn left and walk through a gate to pick up the Toyon Trail (2.5 miles total). Stay on this singletrack trail with views, rolling hills, and periods of shade for 0.6 mile. Exit a gate to arrive at a four-way junction. Take a wide right to pick up the Bay View Trail away from Garrod Farms. (Alternatively, you can just remain on the Toyon Trail for the next 0.4 mile.)

You're now on a fire trail, and from here on out, you'll be going mostly flat or downhill. This stretch has nice views of the Santa Clara Valley and the Diablo Range. At 3.5 miles, turn right at a junction for the Toyon Trail. Soon after, turn left at a T following a sign for Prospect Road Parking. Stay on the Toyon Trail until 3.8 miles total, enjoying more valley views. As you return to the junction with the Hayfield Trail, turn right and continue 0.4 mile to a T, where you turn right again. In a few hundred yards, at another T with the Seven Springs Loop Trail, turn right. When you reach the Cora Older Trail on your left, take it. Descend more than 200 feet in elevation over 0.4 mile through a mix of shade and sun to reach the Prospect Road parking area.

GO FARTHER

For another hike with a similar difficulty level in this preserve, hike to Rainbow Knoll and Hunter's Point via the Seven Springs Loop Trail.

MAKE IT SHORTER

Families can do a 1.8-mile out-and-back visit to Hunter's Point with under 300 feet of elevation gain. From this scenic lookout, you can take in views of the Santa Clara Valley.

Next page: Second-growth redwood trees are a common sight on the first part of the route in Sanborn County Park (Hike 31).

SARATOGA AND LOS GATOS

This chapter explores the magical area near Saratoga and Los Gatos, to the south and east of State Route 9 (Big Basin Way), and on either side of State Route 17. In this perfect mix of town and country, you'll visit two more developed parks and spend the rest of the time deep in nature.

While many flock to Saratoga's Montalvo Arts Center for a picnic on its expansive lawn, you'll circle the center's trails, enjoying art installations, redwoods, and a scenic viewpoint. An equally popular Saratoga park with a completely different vibe is the cool and shaded Sanborn County Park. Here you'll hike the park's family-friendly and self-guided Nature Trail before taking a climb into the hills.

In neighboring Los Gatos, you'll find a fitness lovers' paradise in St. Joseph's Hill, with trails above Lexington Reservoir and around a former Jesuit school and winery. Then, you'll head south on State Route 17 to explore Bear Creek Redwoods Open Space Preserve, where you'll hike a peaceful loop around redwoods (including some impressive old-growth ones) and Douglas-firs.

The chapter concludes with a visit to Castle Rock State Park, which features several sandstone formations, including the large and impressive Castle Rock. Here you'll hike among rock climbers while you take in expansive views of the Santa Cruz Mountains and the ocean.

30 Montalvo Arts Center

DISTANCE: 2.3 miles
ELEVATION GAIN: 640 feet
HIGH POINT: 1,160 feet
DIFFICULTY: Moderate
TIME: 1 hour and 15 minutes
FITNESS: Hikers, fit walkers. The route has both steep uphills and downhills.
FAMILY-FRIENDLY: Families can visit the Nature Trail, Creek Trail, or part of the North Orchard Trail for something less steep.
DOG-FRIENDLY: Yes, on leash on the trails. Dogs are not allowed in the botanical gardens or the villa.
AMENITIES: Restrooms, benches, gardens, art installations, lawn for picnicking
CONTACT: Santa Clara County Parks
BEFORE YOU GO: Hikers should park in parking lot 4. Bring lunch for a picnic.
GPS: 37° 14' 38.6916" N, 122° 1' 45.9912" W

GETTING THERE

Map to: Villa Montalvo lot 4, 15400 Montalvo Road, Saratoga.
Parking: Free parking. Hikers should park in lot 4.

Named after sixteenth-century Spanish writer Garci Ordóñez (or Rodríguez) de Montalvo, who coined the name "California," the Montalvo Arts Center is home to the Lucas Artists Program, a creative incubator that commissions art and hosts festivals, exhibits, and other programming. On the center's 175-acre grounds, you'll find temporary and permanent installations, artists' residences, a lawn for picnicking, hiking trails, and a 1912 villa built for former banker and three-time San Francisco mayor James Phelan.

This route takes you on a short but comprehensive tour of the grounds. There are many twists and turns, so read the directions closely. What the hike lacks in distance, it makes

up for in sights, including oak and bay laurel trees, redwood groves, art installations, and a viewpoint looking over San Jose and the South Bay. Note that this is no flat walk in the park—to get to the viewpoint, you'll need to gain over 600 feet of elevation.

GET MOVING

Note: Most distances on this route are under 0.2 mile. In this write-up, I'll only call out distances over 0.2 mile. Otherwise, I'll just note junction numbers.

From parking lot 4, pick up the Lookout Trail and head uphill. This singletrack trail is lined by bay laurels, eucalyptus, toyon,

The Montalvo Arts Center is a unique art-filled walk with a stunning viewpoint.

poison oak, and ferns. When you reach junction 23, head left at the domed Belvedere Temple to stay on the Lookout Trail toward the Nature Trail. Then at junction 22, turn right on the Nature Trail toward the Carriage House Trail.

At junction 21, take a sharp left and head uphill on the Carriage House Trail. On this stretch, you'll come upon a sign reading "Sky Trees Leaves Earth," the first of several meditative prompts on this route. These are part of *A Healing Walk*, a work by Bay Area artist and curator Susan O'Malley. Part of the center's permanent collection, this work prompts us to be mindful and appreciate our time in nature.

When you reach junction 20, turn right on the Redwood Trail toward the Poet's Walk. At the Poet's Walk, continue to junction 14, where you turn right on the Redwood Trail toward the Creek Trail. On this stretch, you'll take redwood-lined switchbacks down to a creek. At junction 3, cross a bridge and turn left to stay on the Creek Trail toward the North Orchard Trail. This bridge marks the start of artist and composer Howard Hersh's *Four Bridges* sound installation, where you use your mobile phone to listen to a curated collection of music, animal and nature sounds, children's voices and laughter, and poems for a 26-minute-plus immersive ambulatory experience, available on the Montalvo Arts Center app. Some content may not be suitable for children.

When you arrive at junction 4, make a right on the North Orchard Trail toward the South Orchard Trail. Then, when you quickly reach junction 5, bear right on the North Orchard Trail toward Norton Road. Cross the second of Hersh's bridges here and enter an exposed area where you'll pass by artist residences. Close to the end of this stretch, you'll pass over the third of Hersh's bridges. You soon come to junction 6, where you turn left to stay on the North Orchard Trail toward the South Orchard Trail. Shortly after this, cross the fourth of Hersh's bridges.

When you reach junction 7, stay straight on the North Orchard Trail. Then, at junction 10, bear right on the North Orchard Trail toward the Lookout Trail. Stay here until you reach junction 11, where you turn right to pick up the Lookout Trail heading toward the Lookout Point Trail junction. Climb some stairs and cross a bridge. You'll be on this stretch for 0.3 mile. Partway through this section, you'll come upon a peaceful redwood grove.

At junction 25 at a small clearing, head straight on the Lookout Trail toward parking lot 3. When you arrive at junction 24, turn right and head uphill on the Lookout Trail. You're now on a 0.6-mile roundtrip visit to and from Lookout Point.

From this viewpoint (which has two benches), enjoy views of San Jose, Moffett Field, Mount Hamilton, Mission Peak, and more. After taking in the views, head back 0.3 mile to junction 24, where you'll head straight and downhill on the Lookout Trail for another 0.3 mile. At junction 22, turn right to stay on the Lookout Trail, and at the Belvedere Temple, head right to parking lot 4.

MAKE IT SHORTER

This is already a short route, but hikers can cut down on the distance even further by taking the Lookout Trail from lot 4 and heading directly to the Lookout Point. You arrive in just 0.7 mile (1.4 miles roundtrip).

GO FARTHER

Make a day of it! Bring a picnic lunch to enjoy on the lawn. Then take a walk to explore the art and gardens.

31 Sanborn County Park

DISTANCE: 3.4 miles
ELEVATION GAIN: 750 feet
HIGH POINT: 2,020 feet
DIFFICULTY: Moderate
TIME: 1 hour and 30 minutes
FITNESS: Hikers, walkers, runners. Walkers can skip the hill for an easier walk.
FAMILY-FRIENDLY: Families can walk the 0.7-mile Nature Trail (see Make It Shorter).
DOG-FRIENDLY: Yes, on leash
AMENITIES: Restrooms, ranger station, benches, amphitheater, campgrounds, picnic areas, historic sites
CONTACT: Santa Clara County Parks
BEFORE YOU GO: Pick up a Nature Trail brochure at the ranger station on your way into the park.
GPS: 37° 14' 5.9496" N, 122° 3' 43.83" W

GETTING THERE

Map to: 16055 Sanborn Road, Saratoga. **Parking:** Park in the sizable Sequoia parking lot. There is a small parking fee payable at the ranger station; cash and credit cards are accepted.

Walden Pond is part of the "Walden West" estate established by uranium miner Vernon J. Pick, who named it in honor of Henry David Thoreau.

Sanborn County Park is a local favorite. The selected route includes a tour around the 0.7-mile Nature Trail plus a jaunt into the hills, including a steep mile-long incline. The densely forested Nature Trail offers a self-guided tour with fourteen points of interest on the trail's flora, fauna, and local history. Pick up a brochure at the ranger station before hiking.

Venturing beyond the Nature Trail, you'll circle Walden Pond—part of the larger "Walden West" estate established by Vernon J. Pick, a uranium miner who bought and lived on this land, built an electronics and geology laboratory here, and named it for his hero, Henry David Thoreau. You'll also climb some 600 feet of elevation on a trail named after Pick. The tall redwoods and Douglas-firs throughout this park leave you with no real views, but this is a perfect place to escape the heat on warm days.

GET MOVING

From the Sequoia parking area, head right at a sign for the Sequoia Group Area. After 100 feet, turn left at a sign for the Peterson and Nature Trails. Arrive at the restrooms after 275 feet and turn left on a paved road, following a sign for the Nature Trail. Then, shortly after, make a right onto the Nature Trail.

Follow a narrow sidewalk for 100 feet, then make a right, head down some stairs, and use a bridge to cross Aubry Creek. Once across the creek, look for a Nature Trail sign and head up a dirt trail with some stairs. Here you'll see the first of many numbered markers that represent points of interest featured in the Nature Trail brochure.

After 400 feet, follow a sign left to stay on the Nature Trail. Soon after that, turn right at junction 41 to follow the Nature Trail down a flight of stairs. At marker 9 (0.3 mile total), head left at a junction with the Vernon J. Pick Trail. (For a 0.7-mile option from this point, see Make It Shorter.)

Reach junction 36 on the Vernon J. Pick Trail and stay right to stay on this trail. There are two beautiful redwood fairy rings here. When you reach junction 104, pass through a parking lot and pick up the paved San Andreas Connector Trail across the way. At 0.6 mile, reach junction 20 and a T, where you turn right on the San Andreas Connector Trail.

Turn right at junction 19 onto the San Andreas Trail. Then you'll soon make a right on the narrow Walden Pond Connector Trail. Reach a paved road after 200 feet, where you'll make a left and then a quick jog right on a dirt trail that goes around the back of the pond. As you finish your loop around the pond, look for the 1908 Welch-Hurst House off to the right. This was Vernon Pick's former home. Then return to the paved road, stay right, and head uphill on the paved Vernon J. Pick Trail. At 0.9 mile, stay straight on the Vernon J. Pick Trail at junction 32. Continue uphill for half a mile.

At junction 15, head straight and continue uphill on the dirt Upper Madrone Trail. Then at 1.8 miles, turn left at junction 14

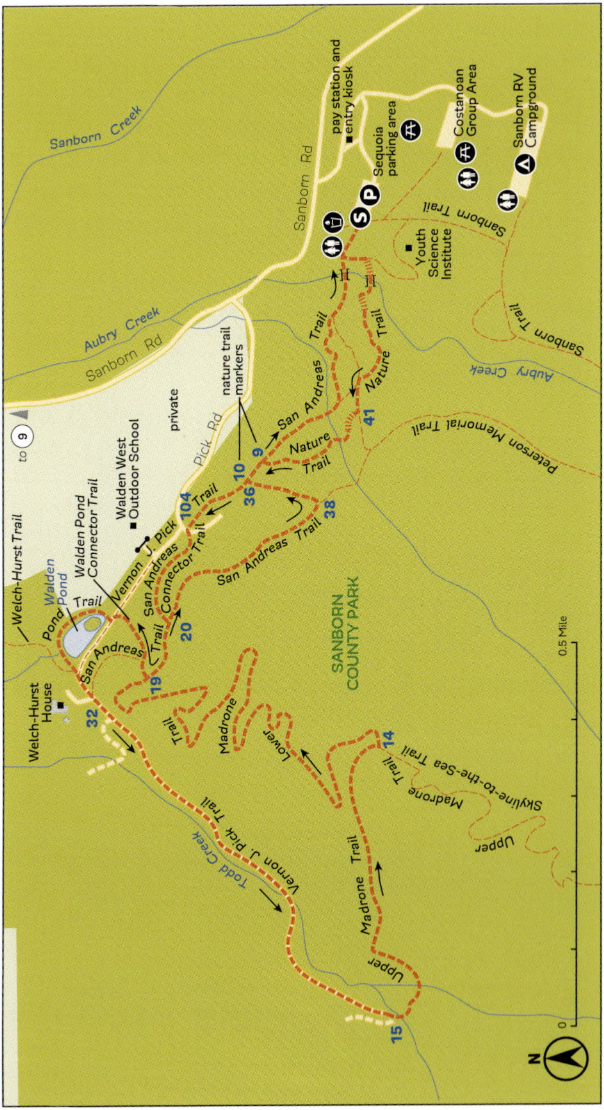
Sanborn Creek
Aubry Creek
Sanborn Rd
pay station and entry kiosk
Sequoia parking area
Costanoan Group Area
Sanborn RV Campground
Sanborn Trail
Youth Science Institute
Nature Trail
San Andreas Trail
Peterson Memorial Trail
nature trail markers
private
Pick Rd
Walden West Outdoor School
Walden Pond Connector Trail
Welch-Hurst Trail
Walden Pond
Pond Trail
Vernon J. Pick Trail
San Andreas Connector Trail
San Andreas Trail
SANBORN COUNTY PARK
Welch-Hurst House
Madrone Trail
Lower Madrone Trail
Upper Madrone Trail
Skyline-to-the-Sea Trail
Todd Creek
to 9
9
10
36
38
41
104
20
19
32
14
15
0
0.5 Mile
N

onto the Lower Madrone Trail, a narrow dirt trail with switchbacks. Descend for 0.6 mile, then continue straight at junction 19 and straight again at junction 20. Walk through an open area for 0.2 mile to junction 38, where you turn left. Turn right at junction 36 to pick up the Nature Trail toward the visitor center. After 125 feet, stay straight. You'll see marker 10 ahead of you at 2.8 miles total.

Walk past marker 10, and after 0.1 mile, stay left at a sign for the Nature Trail. Then, in another 0.1 mile, bear left, cross a bridge, and return to the restrooms and parking lot where you started.

MAKE IT SHORTER

The Nature Trail is 0.7 mile and has 100 feet of elevation gain. To hike this route, follow the write-up above through marker 9 and then take a right and return to your vehicle.

32 St. Joseph's Hill Open Space Preserve

DISTANCE: 3.9 miles
ELEVATION GAIN: 800 feet
HIGH POINT: 1,253 feet
DIFFICULTY: Moderate
TIME: 1 hour and 45 minutes
FITNESS: Hikers, fit walkers, runners
FAMILY-FRIENDLY: Due to the elevation gain, this route is best for families with older children.
DOG-FRIENDLY: Yes
AMENITIES: A few benches along the route
CONTACT: Midpeninsula Regional Open Space District (St. Joseph's Hill Open Space Preserve) and Town of Los Gatos (Novitiate Park)
BEFORE YOU GO: There are no restrooms, so stop in town or at the Lexington Reservoir parking area.
GPS: 37° 12' 54.918" N, 121° 59' 6.9576" W

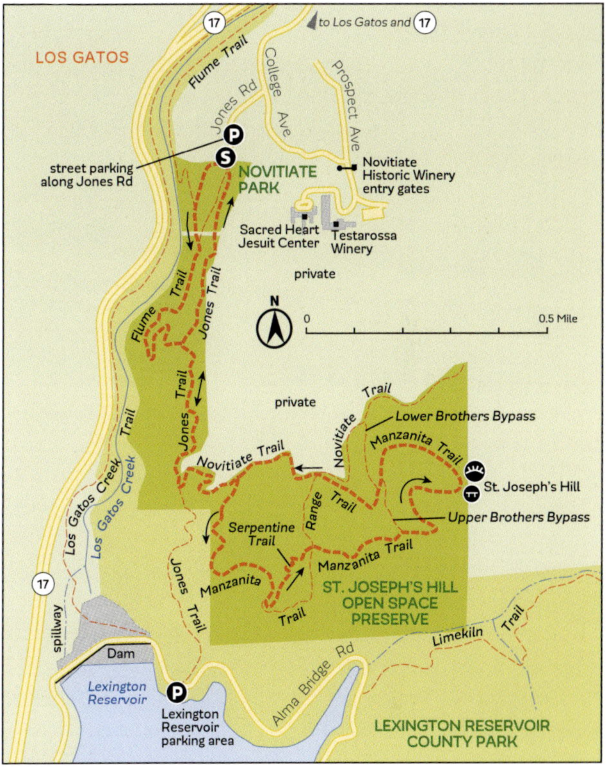

GETTING THERE

Map to: Jones Creek Trail Entrance, 216-298 Jones Road, Los Gatos. **Public Transit:** VTA bus 27 stops at Main Street and Los Gatos Civic Center, 0.7 mile from the hike start. **Parking:** Street parking is available along Jones Road.

St. Joseph's Hill Open Space Preserve is a fitness super-highway where hikers, bikers, runners, and their dogs are living their best lives out in nature. In 1888, the Jesuits operated a training school (or novitiate) and winery on this land.

The remnants of two ghost towns, Lexington and Alma, now lie submerged beneath Lexington Reservoir.

The novitiate closed in 1967 and is now a retirement home for priests. The winery is now Testarossa Winery. In 1982, Los Gatos and the Midpeninsula Regional Open Space District acquired the land.

Starting with a short segment in Novitiate Park, you'll quickly enter St. Joseph's Hill Open Space Preserve and do a loop around this park. The crowds thin out as you head uphill, taking in views of Lexington Reservoir and Mount Umunhum, walking through serpentine grasslands, and exploring narrow trails lined with manzanita trees. From 1,253-foot-tall St. Joseph's Hill, you'll enjoy panoramic views of the Santa Clara Valley. Then you'll head downhill, taking a few more trails back to the start.

GET MOVING

Starting at the entrance to Novitiate Park, take the farthest right of three trails. After 0.2 mile, enter St. Joseph's Hill Open Space Preserve, where you take the Flume Trail, a singletrack dirt trail that enters the woods. On the left of this narrow trail is an exposed rock face. On the right, there's a steep drop-off and the sights and sounds of State Route 17.

Poison oak and bay laurel, oak, scrub oak, and manzanita trees line the trail. When you reach a junction at 0.6 mile, turn right on the Jones Trail toward the Novitiate Trail and Alma Bridge Road. The Jones Trail is a wide fire road with larger oak trees to the left and manzanita trees to the right. It follows the route of an old stagecoach road that connected Los Gatos to Lexington and Alma, two ghost towns now submerged by the Lexington Reservoir.

At 1 mile, turn left on the Novitiate Trail toward the Manzanita Trail and the Hilltop Vista. At 1.2 miles, turn right, following a sign for the Manzanita Trail to Hilltop Vista. From this trail, you'll see Lexington Reservoir below and to your right. The Santa Clara Valley Water District built this reservoir in 1952 for the local water supply, but now it's a popular spot for hiking, running, boating, stand-up paddleboarding, and fishing.

At 1.6 miles, reach an intersection with the Serpentine Trail. For a change of pace, stay left at the fork to pick up this singletrack trail. To start, you're surrounded on both sides by manzanita trees. Then, the trail opens up to a clearing with grass and wildflowers in spring. On clear days, you can see Mount Diablo and Mission Peak.

After 0.2 mile on the Serpentine Trail (1.8 miles total), reach a four-way intersection. Continue straight to get back onto the Manzanita Trail toward the Hilltop Vista. Continue on the Manzanita Trail for half a mile, ignoring the Upper Brothers Bypass Trail on your left. As you climb toward the Hilltop Vista, take a look at the reservoir and then walk through grasslands. At the end of this stretch, look for Mount Umunhum. At the 1,253-foot summit of St. Joseph's Hill, there are views of the Santa Clara Valley and a bench to relax on.

When you're ready, start your 1.6-mile descent. About 300 feet after the summit, enter a small, shaded oak grove, which is a nice respite on hot days. As you leave the grove, take in sweeping views to the north and east.

At 2.6 miles, pass the Upper Brothers Bypass Trail on the left. Then 300 feet later, pass the Lower Brothers Bypass Trail on the right. When you reach a four-way intersection 0.2 mile after this, stay straight on the Novitiate Trail. Continue half a mile, passing the Manzanita Trail on your left halfway through this stretch.

At the Jones Trail intersection, make a sharp right and take this trail a final 0.8 mile back to the hike start. There can be speedy cyclists on this trail. If this bothers you, turn left after 0.3 mile to take the Flume Trail the rest of the way.

GO FARTHER

For flatter alternatives to this route, check out the trails in Lexington Reservoir County Park and Vasona Lake County Park or the paved and accessible Los Gatos Creek Trail.

33 Bear Creek Redwoods Open Space Preserve

DISTANCE: 5.5 miles
ELEVATION GAIN: 1,110 feet
HIGH POINT: 1,890 feet
DIFFICULTY: Challenging
TIME: 2 hours and 30 minutes
FITNESS: Hikers, walkers, runners. Walkers can walk to the old-growth redwoods 1.4 miles into the hike and turn around.
FAMILY-FRIENDLY: See above.
DOG-FRIENDLY: No
AMENITIES: Restrooms, picnic areas, accessible trails, historic sites (see Go Farther)
CONTACT: Midpeninsula Regional Open Space District
BEFORE YOU GO: On warm days, San Cruz beach traffic on State Route 17 can slow your arrival to the park.
GPS: 37° 10' 57.7524" N, 122° 0' 14.4324" W

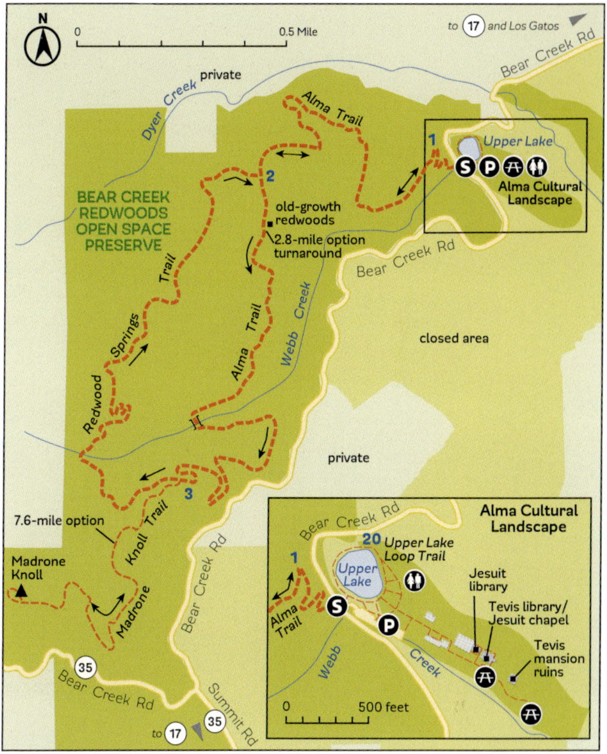

GETTING THERE

Map to: Bear Creek Redwoods Alma parking area, Los Gatos. **Parking:** There are fifty standard spaces and three ADA spaces in the lot off Bear Creek Road. Note: Parking can fill up fast. Arrive early or come in the afternoon after the morning hikers are gone.

Opened in 2019, Bear Creek Redwoods Open Space Preserve is one of the Bay Area's newer parks. It was almost developed into a golf course and country club, but environmental

Among the few towering old-growth redwoods in this preserve, you'll find this one with a burl supporting its own tree.

activists fought to save the land, and the Midpeninsula Regional Open Space District and the Peninsula Open Space Trust ultimately acquired it.

As the name indicates, you'll see redwoods in this park, but you'll also see bay laurels, Douglas-firs, and various other flora, including colorful wildflowers. If you're mostly here for the redwoods, know that most are found along the Alma Trail, and the best ones are in the first 2 miles of this route. For me, the park's highlights are the small stand of old-growth redwoods 1.4 miles into the route and a bridge over Webb Creek at just under 2 miles. As this route is mostly forested, it's a great escape on hot days. However, since the preserve is close to CA-17, these are the exact days you'll need to watch out for Santa Cruz beach traffic slowing travel to the park.

GET MOVING

From the parking lot, walk to Bear Creek Road and cross the street using the signal button. There's one button at human height and another button for people on horseback! Pick up the Alma Trail. You immediately enter the woods and start heading uphill on a wide fire trail. You'll see redwoods and also low-lying plants such as blackberry, coastal hedgenettle, and poison oak. After 0.2 mile of switchbacks, reach junction 1, where you turn left to stay on the Alma Trail.

You'll be on this trail for another mile. At 0.6 mile, you can see Mount Thayer and its towers on your right. At 0.7 mile, stay on the wide trail when you see a turnoff on the left. And at 0.9 mile, follow the trail as it bends left. To the right is a preserve boundary. When you reach junction 2 at 1.2 miles, stay straight on the Alma Trail, where you'll hike for the next 1.5 miles (until 2.7 miles total). My two favorite spots in this preserve are found in the first half of this long segment.

First, just 0.2 mile into this stretch, you arrive at a stand of a few old-growth redwoods. There's one double redwood with one trunk and two tops, and there's another with a seemingly full-sized redwood growing upward from an oddly shaped dangling burl. At 2 miles, reach a bridge over Webb Creek. The light filtering onto this bridge surrounded by redwoods creates a serene atmosphere. At 2.2 miles, follow the trail right (the area to the left is off limits). Then, shortly after this, you can see a metal tower with a white sphere on top of it in the distance. This is the Next Generation Weather Radar (NEXRAD) station on Mount Umunhum.

At 2.7 miles, reach a three-way intersection at junction 3 (see Go Farther if you'd like to add 2.1 miles to your hike from this point). Continue straight at this junction to pick up the Redwood Springs Trail. You'll be on this trail for a total of 1.6 miles (until 4.3 miles total). Pass through some redwoods, Douglas-firs, and some exposed areas. About half a mile into this stretch, you'll cross Webb Creek again. You may encounter some wet patches on the trail, and you'll hear the creek below you. At 4.3 miles, you're back at junction 2. Make a left on the Alma Trail and follow the trail back to Bear Creek Road and the parking area.

GO FARTHER

For a longer hike, take the Madrone Knoll Trail up to Madrone Knoll from junction 3 for a 7.6-mile hike with 1,650 feet of elevation gain. Note: There are no significant changes in scenery or views here, just more mileage and elevation.

MAKE IT SHORTER

Just want to see the best redwoods on the route? Turn around at 1.4 miles for a 2.8-mile hike with 700 feet of elevation gain.

For shorter hike options, you can get a park brochure and explore the flat and accessible 0.2-mile Upper Lake Loop Trail. You can also visit the former library and chapel of Alma College, the first Jesuit school of theology on the West Coast. The ruins of a mansion located just beyond the chapel is now a bat habitat. The mansion once belonged to Dr. Harry Lloyd Tevis, whose father, banker and financier Lloyd Tevis, made his fortune in railroads, mining, and real estate. Harry Tevis owned the land before the Jesuits bought it in 1934.

34 Castle Rock State Park

DISTANCE:	5.7 miles
ELEVATION GAIN:	1,150 feet
HIGH POINT:	3,170 feet
DIFFICULTY:	Moderate to challenging
TIME:	3 hours
FITNESS:	Hikers, walkers, runners. Walkers can head directly to Castle Rock (0.6 mile from main parking lot).
FAMILY-FRIENDLY:	See above.
DOG-FRIENDLY:	No
AMENITIES:	Restrooms, ranger station, pay phone, picnic sites, water, EV charging
CONTACT:	California State Parks
BEFORE YOU GO:	Don't miss the views—this park is best on a clear day! Also, don't be alarmed by the sound of gunshots; the Los Altos Rod and Gun Club range is just north of here.
GPS:	37° 13' 55.8336" N, 122° 5' 53.898" W

GETTING THERE

Map to: Castle Rock State Park parking. **Parking:** The main parking lot has over fifty parking spaces, including ADA spaces, and there is an overflow lot 0.3 mile south. Pay the parking fee by cash or card before hiking.

Popular among rock climbers, 5,200-acre Castle Rock State Park also has much to offer hikers. You'll enjoy jaw-dropping views of the Santa Cruz Mountains, the ocean, and all the way down to Monterey. You'll also see large tafoni sandstone formations and a waterfall. There is some class 1 and 2 rock scrambling and one short and easy section with metal cables, so come prepared with good footwear. This route combines the Ridge Trail's oak woodlands and Goat Rock Overlook and the

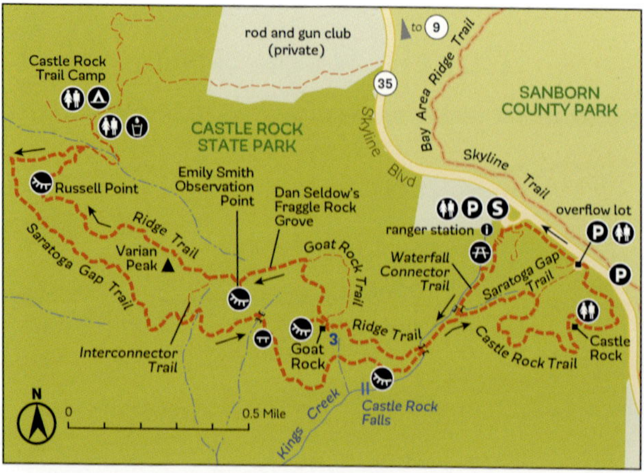

Saratoga Gap Trail's stunning views and Castle Rock Falls. At the end of the route, you'll visit Castle Rock, the park's eponymous tafoni rock formation you can climb on and around.

GET MOVING

From the main parking lot, pass the ranger station and descend a small set of stairs. At the bottom of the stairs, head right on the Waterfall Connector Trail. Pass an area with benches and a statue of a redwood's roots, then continue straight on the Waterfall Connector Trail toward some informational signage. You soon enter the woods. At 0.3 mile, cross a wooden bridge and turn right on the Saratoga Gap Trail toward the Ridge Trail. Then at 0.4 mile, cross a creek using a smaller wood bridge and head straight to pick up the Ridge Trail toward Goat Rock.

On this stretch, you get your first glimpses of tafoni sandstone, and then you'll emerge from the woods to get your first views. You'll also do some class 1 and 2 scrambling around large sandstone formations. There are some side trails with dead-ends here. If your trail peters out, return to where you last knew you were on the trail to get back on the route.

The park's namesake rock is 60 feet tall and features caves and rare tafoni formations.

At 0.8 mile, reach a trail marker pointing right. Shortly after this, arrive at Goat Rock, where you stay right. Continue on the Ridge Trail. The trail splits shortly after Goat Rock. At marker 3, head left and continue to the Goat Rock Overlook for stunning Santa Cruz Mountain views. Then return to marker 3 (1 mile total) and take a left on the Ridge Trail toward Castle Rock Trail Camp.

Continue mostly downhill on the Ridge Trail for 1.2 more miles (until 2.2 miles total). You can head to Dan Seldow's Fraggle Rock Grove 0.2 mile into this stretch and the Emily Smith Observation Point 0.1 mile later (not included in route mileage). Then, shortly after the Observation Point, pass the Interconnector Trail and continue 0.8 mile farther to a trail marker for the Castle Rock Trail Camp. If you need a restroom or water, continue straight here toward the trail camp. Otherwise, take a sharp left to pick up the Saratoga Gap Trail.

Hike 1.8 miles on the Saratoga Gap Trail, ignoring the Interconnector Trail after just under 1 mile. The narrow trail is lined with toyons and manzanitas and offers showstopping panoramic views of the Santa Cruz Mountains and the ocean. For short stretches, you'll do some class 1 and 2 scrambling. You'll also encounter a short and easy section with metal cables. This stretch trends uphill, gaining about 300 feet of elevation.

At 4 miles, reach Castle Rock Falls and the Falls Overlook—not the largest of waterfalls, but worth a look since you're here! Then, at 4.2 miles, reach the junction with the Ridge Trail where you were earlier. Head right to cross the small wood bridge and then turn left to stay on the Saratoga Gap Trail. Continue to the larger bridge you encountered previously, but do not cross it; instead stay straight on the Saratoga Gap Trail toward Castle Rock.

After a quarter mile, turn right on the Castle Rock Trail. Follow an arrow left after 0.3 mile and then head left again after another 0.2 mile. Just a few hundred feet later, you'll reach Castle Rock, an impressively large sandstone formation and this park's namesake. You can climb on and around this feature.

To get back to the parking lot, follow the trail sign to the right beyond the rock, then shortly after, follow the sign toward the parking lot. There is also a restroom here. At 5.3 miles, turn left to stay on the Castle Rock Trail, then at 5.5 miles, reach a sign for the parking lot. Head left to reach the lot and a restroom. Head left behind the restroom to take a connector trail for the final 0.2 mile to the main parking lot.

GO FARTHER

Explore part of the Skyline-to-the-Sea Trail. This 30-mile trail starts in Castle Rock Park and goes all the way to Big Basin Redwoods State Park.

MAKE IT SHORTER

Instead of taking a longer trek on the Ridge and Saratoga Gap Trails, head directly to Castle Rock to make the park's eponymous rock formation the main attraction.

Next page: The Halls Valley in Joseph D. Grant County Park (Hike 41) extends between two ridges in the Diablo Range.

SAN JOSE AND MILPITAS

There's a surprising amount of hiking to do in a city of one million people. You'll travel to remote-feeling parks, tackle two urban hiking routes, and explore three of the four longest routes in this book.

You'll start at Santa Teresa County Park, where the aptly named Rocky Ridge Trail takes you to Coyote Peak's 360-degree views. Then you'll hike Alum Rock Park up to Eagle Rock, along Penitencia Creek, past mineral springs ruins, and across ridgelines. Just north of Alum Rock is Sierra Vista Open Space Preserve. Here you'll wander pristine grasslands with stellar views of San Jose, Alum Rock, and the South Bay.

Next are two urban hikes: one around the Evergreen neighborhood and Montgomery Hill, famous for its part in the history of human flight. Then there's Communications Hill, which may lack in distance but more than makes up for it in views.

In Almaden Quicksilver County Park, you'll explore the history and ruins of a former mercury mining area while walking through grasslands with expansive views. Then you'll hike three long routes. In Joseph D. Grant County Park, a 7.4-mile route guides you up to a 2,460-foot-tall viewpoint over the entire Santa Clara Valley and down through the Halls Valley. On the 8.1-mile Mount Umunhum route, you'll learn the history of a former Air Force station and a sacred Amah Mutsun Ohlone site. And on the 8.5-mile Monument Peak route, you'll enjoy views of the Santa Clara Valley that get better and better as you climb.

Be sure to check out Appendix II, which provides a table of additional trails in San Jose, many of them flat and running along local creeks. These don't require turn-by-turn directions but are meant to inspire further exploration.

35 Santa Teresa County Park

DISTANCE: 3.7 miles
ELEVATION GAIN: 740 feet
HIGH POINT: 1,160 feet
DIFFICULTY: Moderate
TIME: 1 hour and 45 minutes
FITNESS: Hikers, fit walkers, runners
FAMILY-FRIENDLY: This route is best for families with older children due to the elevation gain.
DOG-FRIENDLY: Yes, on leash (except at the Bernal-Gulnac-Joice Ranch mentioned in Go Farther)
AMENITIES: Restrooms, benches, picnic areas
CONTACT: Santa Clara County Parks
BEFORE YOU GO: This route has little shade and is best in spring. Avoid for a few days after winter rains, as trails can be muddy. If you have balance issues, the aptly named Rocky Ridge Trail may not be suitable for you. Bring poles for stability. Bikers love these trails; watch out for their speedy descents. Because planes fly overhead frequently, it's not the quietest trail, but the views are worth it!
GPS: 37° 12' 46.1088" N, 121° 47' 15.6372" W

GETTING THERE

Map to: Pueblo day use area, San Jose. **Parking:** Park in one of the lots at the Pueblo Entrance. I recommend parking by the restroom. Make sure to pay at the kiosk before you start hiking.

It's hard to pack more adventure into a 3.7-mile route just twenty minutes from downtown San Jose. Here you'll climb antenna-topped Coyote Peak via the Rocky Ridge Trail. I've hiked all over the Bay Area, and the plethora of rocks scattered across this trail give it a truly unique feel.

Let's face it: You're probably coming here for views! Looking north from 1,155-foot Coyote Peak, you can see San Jose and the Santa Clara Valley. And on clear days, you can see as far north as San Francisco and Mount Tamalpais. To the west, you'll see Mount Umunhum and Loma Prieta, and to the east, you'll feel like you're having a stare-down with Mount Hamilton. You'll get views of the Coyote Valley, Morgan Hill, and Gilroy to the south. On the way down from the peak, you'll return to the start via the peaceful Hidden Springs Trail.

GET MOVING

Start your hike by the restrooms at the Pueblo Entrance. Walk behind the restrooms to pick up the Mine Trail that parallels the parking lot. Turn right and after 0.1 mile, reach a T and head left to continue on the Mine Trail. Just steps into the trail, you can see Mount Umunhum in the distance.

In Santa Teresa County Park, you can hike among the cows within San Jose's city limits.

Stay straight to pick up the Rocky Ridge Trail as the Mine Trail bends right. You'll be on this trail for 1.8 miles (until 2 miles total). At about 0.8 mile total, you start to see where the trail gets its name, as there are rocks of all sizes on the path. Walk through a cattle gate at 0.9 mile. As you climb through grasslands, you can see Loma Prieta in the distance to your right, Mount Hamilton and Mission Peak in the distance to your left, and Coyote Peak and its antenna in the midground. As you reach the end of this stretch, look north to see San Francisco and Mount Tamalpais.

At 2 miles, turn left when you reach the Coyote Peak Trail after you pass a bench. You're now back on a wider gravel trail. Here you see a hill with a round top off to the right called El Toro. This hill is part of the logo of the city of Morgan Hill.

After 0.4 mile on the Coyote Peak Trail (2.4 miles total), reach a junction with the Peak Trail. Stay straight on the Peak Trail here to explore the Coyote Peak vista point with panoramic views of the South Bay, the Peninsula, San Francisco, Marin, Mount Umunhum, Loma Prieta, the Coyote Valley, Mount Hamilton, Mission Peak, and more. There is a 0.1-mile loop trail here, so you can take in views from every angle. And there are benches and garbage cans here, so it's a great place to stop for a snack or lunch.

When you're done taking in the views, head back to the Coyote Peak Trail and turn right. You are heading downhill on a wide dirt trail. Exit a cattle gate at 2.9 miles and take a left onto the Hidden Springs Trail (also the Bay Area Ridge Trail). Continue downhill on the wide dirt trail here 0.5 mile, passing an intersection with the Ridge Trail on the right after 0.3 mile. When you arrive at a parking lot, stay left, following a sign for the Bay Area Ridge Trail. This trail (also the Mine Trail) will take you back to the restroom and the end of the route.

GO FARTHER

Take a self-guided walk around the historic Bernal-Gulnac-Joice Ranch and Santa Teresa Spring.

36 Alum Rock Park

DISTANCE: 6.3 miles
ELEVATION GAIN: 1,080 feet
HIGH POINT: 1,160 feet
DIFFICULTY: Moderate
TIME: 2 hours and 45 minutes
FITNESS: Hikers, runners. Walkers can see Make It Shorter.
FAMILY-FRIENDLY: Families can see Make It Shorter.
DOG-FRIENDLY: No
AMENITIES: Restrooms, benches, picnic areas, ranger station, pay phones, water
CONTACT: City of San Jose
BEFORE YOU GO: This park opens at 8 AM
GPS: 37° 23' 37.158" N, 121° 48' 55.44" W

GETTING THERE

Map to: Eagle Rock parking, Penitencia Creek Road, San Jose. **Public Transit:** VTA bus 71 stops at White Road and Fiji Drive, 1.2 miles from the park entrance. **Parking:** Park in the Eagle

Rock or Rustic Lands lots. If these are full, there are several other lots around the park. Parking is free most days except for holidays. Please check the signs in the lot.

Alum Rock Park is a fitness-focused Disneyland where San Jose comes to celebrate the outdoors. Trail running, biking, hiking, picnicking—you can do it all here in California's oldest municipal park, which dates back to 1872.

I designed this route to help you explore several areas of the park. You'll take in views from Eagle Rock, walk along Penitencia Creek and the ruins of an old hot springs and health resort, climb and descend switchbacks, and take in views from 1,100 feet and higher on the South Rim Trail. While parts of the route are shaded, some are exposed and can get quite hot in summer. Hike early on warm days.

GET MOVING

Start the hike at the western entrance of the Eagle Rock parking lot. Cross the road and head uphill on the Penitencia Creek Trail (also part of the Bay Area Ridge Trail) at junction 3. After 0.1 mile, turn left on North Rim Trail toward Eagle Rock at junction 4.

At 0.2 mile, turn right on the North Rim Trail at junction 26. Continue another 0.2 mile on the North Rim Trail and head left when the trail splits at junction 27. When you reach a T at 0.5 mile, continue left and uphill. At 0.7 mile, reach Eagle Rock and an overlook with benches. From here, you can see the Eagle Rock parking lot and downtown San Jose, Mount Umunhum, and Loma Prieta.

When you're done taking in the views, head back the way you came. At 0.9 mile, stay straight as a trail branches off to the right. Then, in 150 feet, stay straight on the North Rim Trail at junction 28. Continue on the mostly exposed North Rim Trail for 0.8 mile (until 1.7 miles total), passing junctions 30 (end of

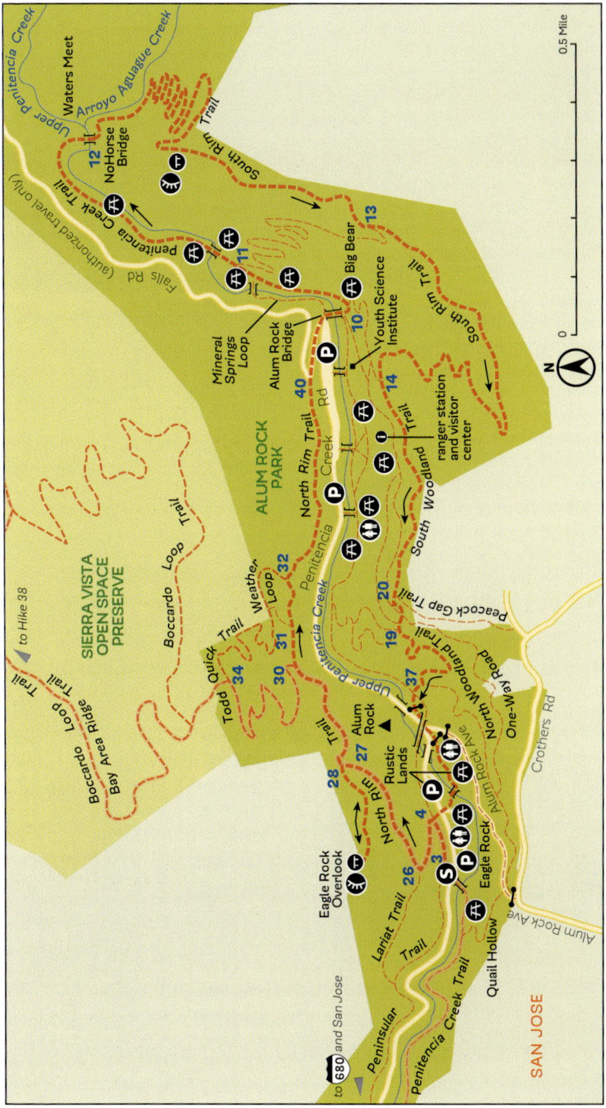
Upper Penitencia Creek
Arroyo Aguague Creek
Waters Meet
NoHorse Bridge
South Rim Trail
Penitencia Creek Trail
Falls Rd (authorized travel only)
Big Bear
Mineral Springs Loop
Alum Rock Bridge
Youth Science Institute
ALUM ROCK PARK
North Rim Trail
Penitencia Creek Rd
ranger station and visitor center
South Woodland Trail
SIERRA VISTA OPEN SPACE PRESERVE
Boccardo Loop Trail
to Hike 38
Todd Quick Trail
Weather Loop
Peacock Gap Trail
North Woodland Trail
One-Way Road
Crothers Rd
Alum Rock Ave
Alum Rock
Rustic Lands
North Rim Trail
Eagle Rock Overlook
Eagle Rock
Lariat Trail
Quail Hollow Trail
Peninsular Trail
Penitencia Creek Trail
to 680 and San Jose
SAN JOSE
Bay Area Ridge Trail
Boccardo Loop Trail
0
0.5 Mile
N

This stone bridge is in an area of the park that once housed a nationally-known health spa with mineral springs.

Bay Area Ridge Trail segment), 31, and 32 along your way. At junction 40, head straight and downhill on the paved trail.

At 1.8 miles, cross the Alum Rock Bridge to reach the Big Bear picnic area. When you get here, look right for a gazebo. This was once a mineral soda fountain (and is just a regular water fountain today). Turn left on the paved Penitencia Creek Trail. The trail is shaded as you approach the historic mineral springs area. Stay on this trail for 0.7 mile, passing junction 11 after 0.3 mile. Partway through this segment, the trail turns back to dirt.

At 2.5 miles, cross the narrow wood and metal NoHorse Bridge and arrive at junction 12. Head uphill, and at 2.7 miles, start just under a mile of shaded switchbacks, where you'll gain about 400 feet of elevation. You'll know you've finished the switchbacks when you exit the shade and reach an overlook with benches. From here, you can see views of San Jose, the South Bay, and the Santa Cruz Mountains.

Continue on a chaparral-lined trail to junction 13 (4 miles total), where you stay left on the South Rim Trail when the trail splits. Then descend 500 feet of elevation over 1.1 miles (until 5.1 miles total) on a shaded, switchback-filled trail. At junction 14, stay straight to pick up the flat South Woodland Trail, which you'll be on for half a mile. At junction 20, continue to a paved service road, then head left. After 150 feet, turn right. Then, after another 25 feet, turn left onto the North Woodland Trail at junction 19.

Head downhill for 0.3 mile and make a right at junction 37 at a sign for the Creek Trail. Continue downhill for 0.1 mile (to 6 miles total), arrive at the Penitencia Creek Trail, and turn left. After 350 feet, exit a gate and head left on a paved trail. Then after another 250 feet, reach street signs for Alum Rock Avenue Penitencia Creek Road. Just to the right of these signs, pass through a gate to enter the Rustic Lands picnic area. Take a wide fire trail for 0.1 mile and cross a bridge at 6.2 miles total. You're back at the Rustic Lands lot, and the Eagle Creek lot is one parking lot over.

GO FARTHER

Head to Sierra Vista Open Space Preserve (Hike 37) for a nearby park with a fraction of the crowds. If you're feeling ambitious, you can access this park via Alum Rock Park's Todd Quick Trail.

MAKE IT SHORTER

For shorter and easier hikes, walkers can hike to Eagle Rock and back following the directions above, or they can explore the flat Penitencia Creek Trail.

37 Sierra Vista Open Space Preserve

DISTANCE: 4.6 miles
ELEVATION GAIN: 980 feet
HIGH POINT: 1,970 feet
DIFFICULTY: Moderate
TIME: 2 hours
FITNESS: Hikers, walkers, runners

FAMILY-FRIENDLY: Families can see Make It Shorter for an easier option.
DOG-FRIENDLY: No
AMENITIES: A few benches along the trail
CONTACT: Santa Clara Valley Open Space Authority
BEFORE YOU GO: It can be very hot here in summer, and there isn't much shade. Come prepared with water and sunscreen. The best time to hike here is in spring when the grass is green and the wildflowers are out.
GPS: 37° 24' 45.6516" N, 121° 47' 1.9032" W

GETTING THERE

Map to: Sierra Vista Open Space Preserve, Sierra Road, San Jose. **Parking:** The Sierra Road staging area has free parking with about forty spaces.

Sierra Vista Open Space Preserve is Alum Rock's quiet neighbor to the north. Alum Rock brings the crowds and the amenities, but Sierra Vista brings the peace. The park is situated at 1,800 feet—a spot so high up and scenic that even its parking lot is known for its views. People come to the lot in droves to enjoy one of the best sunsets in San Jose.

Once you leave the parking area, the crowds thin out. You'll hike through pristine grasslands with sweeping panoramic views. You may see deer or coyotes as well as birds like hawks, vultures, and even bald eagles. The route is rated moderate but can feel challenging on hot days. There is practically no shade, and you'll take on most of the route's elevation (over 600 feet!) in the last 1.7 miles. There's a shortcut in Make It Shorter for an easier route, or you can just pace yourself and soak it all in.

GET MOVING

From the Sierra Road staging area, pick up the Kestrel Trail (part of the Bay Area Ridge Trail) as it passes through a gate and descends through grasslands. Right from the start

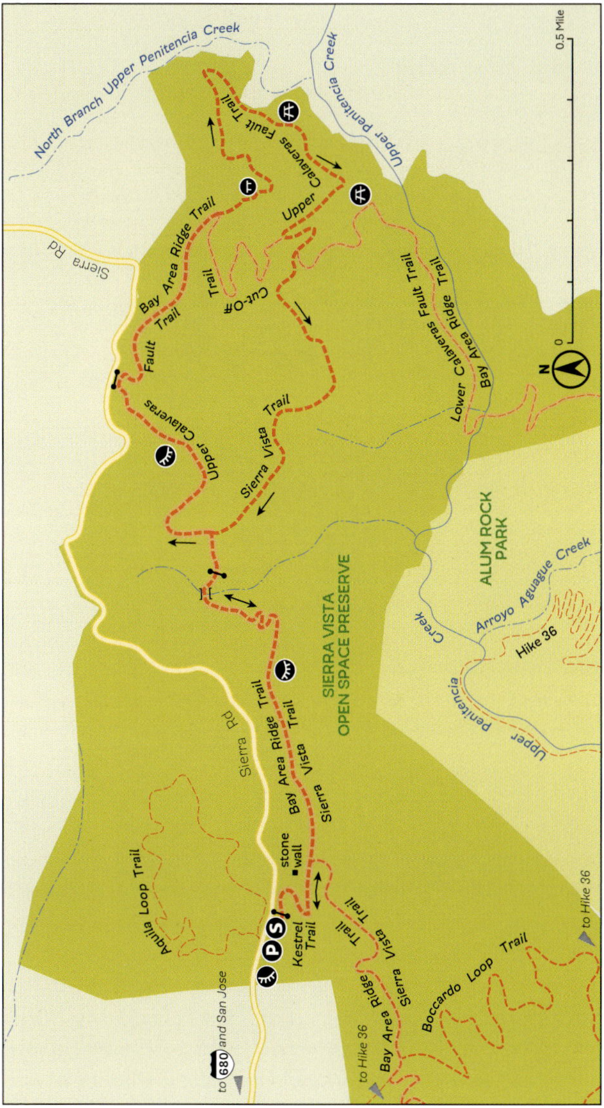
North Branch Upper Penitencia Creek
Upper Penitencia Creek
Sierra Rd
Bay Area Ridge Trail
Fault Trail
Upper Calaveras Fault Trail
Cut-Off Trail
Upper Calaveras
Sierra Vista Trail
Lower Calaveras Fault Trail
Bay Area Ridge Trail
SIERRA VISTA OPEN SPACE PRESERVE
ALUM ROCK PARK
Arroyo Aguague Creek
Hike 36
Upper Penitencia Creek
Aquila Loop Trail
Kestrel Trail
stone wall
Sierra Vista Trail
Bay Area Ridge Trail
Boccardo Loop Trail
to Hike 36
to 680 and San Jose
N
0
0.5 Mile

Come to Sierra Vista for grassy hills dotted with wildflowers and expansive views that start at the parking lot.

of the trail, you can see views of San Jose and the South Bay, Mount Hamilton, and the Lick Observatory. On this stretch, you'll see a stone wall, one of many found across the Bay Area. These walls are of unknown origin and are a Bay Area mystery. You can see another one near the summit of Monument Peak (Hike 43).

After a quarter mile, turn left on the Sierra Vista Trail (also part of the Bay Area Ridge Trail) toward the Upper and Lower Calaveras Fault Trails. Continue descending on a narrow singletrack trail through grasslands. At times on this stretch, there are steep drop-offs to the right of the trail. Here you have views of Alum Rock Park (Hike 39), San Jose, Mount Umunhum (Hike 42), and Loma Prieta.

Just over a mile into the route, turn left on the Upper Calaveras Fault Trail. You know you're getting close to this junction when you cross a bridge and pass through a gate shortly afterward. Over the next half a mile, you'll climb 200 feet in elevation. At the top of the hill, walk through a gate and turn right. Then, descend 200 feet in elevation over 0.3 mile and stay on the Upper Calaveras Fault Trail at a junction with the Cut-Off Trail. (You can also use the Cut-Off Trail to shorten your hike; see Make It Shorter. The Bay Area Ridge Trail also follows the Cut-Off Trail here.)

Stay on the Upper Calaveras Fault Trail for another 0.9 mile. At 0.6 mile into this stretch, there is a picnic bench in the shade. You may also hear a nearby creek flowing during and just after the rainy season. At times, there is a steep drop-off to the left. At 2.8 miles, arrive at the other end of the Cut-Off Trail. Take a hard left and head downhill on the Upper Calaveras Fault Trail. Then, after 0.1 mile, head right and uphill on the Sierra Vista Trail. Pace yourself: This is where your 1.7-mile ascent back to the start begins.

At 3.6 miles, turn left on the Sierra Vista Trail toward the Kestrel and Boccardo Loop Trails. Now you're doubling back on trails you hiked previously. Take the Sierra Vista Trail 0.8 mile, then bear right on the Kestrel Trail and continue a quarter mile to the start.

GO FARTHER

Check out the 4.1-mile Boccardo Loop. This loop trail lets you to connect to Alum Rock Park via the Todd Quick Trail.

MAKE IT SHORTER

For a shorter version of this hike, use the Cut-Off Trail to trim half a mile from your overall distance. You can also do a short 1.1-mile hike on the Aquila Loop Trail.

38 Communications Hill

DISTANCE: 1.7 miles
ELEVATION GAIN: 180 feet
HIGH POINT: 350 feet
DIFFICULTY: Easy
TIME: 45 minutes
FITNESS: Hikers, walkers, runners
FAMILY-FRIENDLY: Yes
DOG-FRIENDLY: Yes, on leash
AMENITIES: Overlooks and benches
CONTACT: City of San Jose
BEFORE YOU GO: The hike begins with nine flights of stairs, so pace yourself. This is a great place to take in a sunset.
GPS: 37° 16' 54.6096" N, 121° 51' 22.356" W

GETTING THERE

Map to: Montevarchi Street and Mullinix Way, San Jose. **Public Transit:** VTA bus 70's Capitol and Copperfield stop is 0.6 mile from the hike start. **Parking:** Free street parking. Park as close as you can to the intersection of Montevarchi Street and Mullinix Way. Make sure to avoid tow-away zones.

The Grand Staircase is the first sight you see on the Communications Hill Trail.

This is the shortest hike in the book, but I wanted to include this route because I hope you'll love urban hiking in neighborhoods as much as I do. This route also gives you expansive views of the Santa Cruz Mountains for just 200 feet of elevation gain. One day, the Communications Hill Trail will be part of a more extensive trail network, but for now, enjoy this quick neighborhood jaunt.

After climbing an elegant staircase, you'll walk the Communications Hill Trail, explore a bit of the Communications Hill neighborhood, and check out the 114-foot-tall brutalist tower that inspired this hill's name. The decommissioned communications tower, known as Oak Hill Tower, was part of the AT&T Long Lines system that used to bring long-distance phone service and television signals across the United States.

GET MOVING

Start the hike at the bottom of the Grand Staircase near the intersection of Montevarchi Street and Mullinix Way. Climb nine flights of steps until you reach a sidewalk, where you turn left. This is the Communications Hill Trail. Pass an overlook on your left and more of the Grand Staircase on your right. Continue on the trail, enjoying sweeping views to the west, including Mount Umunhum and Loma Prieta.

At just under half a mile, head right and climb up four stairs to reach the Vieira Park Outlook. Follow the sidewalk straight through the outlook and then turn right onto Adeline Avenue, which takes you through the Communications Hill neighborhood. (Feel free to take a quick detour into Vieira Park across the street too.)

When you reach Casselino Drive at 0.7 mile, turn right and enjoy expansive westward views interrupted by a short stretch of townhomes. Pass St. Florian Way, then take the next left on Empoli Street for a one-block out-and-back detour to Adeline Avenue, where you'll see Oak Hill Tower. After visiting the tower, head back to Casselino Drive and turn left. In one block, at the intersection of Casselino Drive and Lina Street, catch the views from the top of the Grand Staircase.

Continue on Casselino Drive for 0.3 mile, and when you dead-end into four-lane Communications Hill Boulevard at 1 mile total, you can head left on a sidewalk to extend your walk and get views to the south and east (not included in the route mileage). Or, if you're ready to finish this route, turn right on a wide sidewalk to pick up the Communications Hill Trail. After 500 feet, stay right on the wide paved trail (do not bear left on the narrow sidewalk). Continue back to the Grand Staircase, then descend the stairs to return to the start.

39 Evergreen Urban Hike

DISTANCE:	2.8 miles
ELEVATION GAIN:	260 feet
HIGH POINT:	594 feet
DIFFICULTY:	Easy
TIME:	1 hour and 15 minutes
FITNESS:	Hikers, walkers, runners
FAMILY-FRIENDLY:	Yes
DOG-FRIENDLY:	Yes, on leash
AMENITIES:	Restrooms, water, overlooks, benches, picnic areas
CONTACT:	City of San Jose, Evergreen Valley College
BEFORE YOU GO:	Aside from Montgomery Hill Park, this route is accessible. Go in spring for green grass and wildflowers on Montgomery Hill.
GPS:	37° 17' 51.3384" N, 121° 46' 3.7092" W

GETTING THERE

Map to: Park Estates Way and Royal Estate Court. **Public Transit:** VTA buses 31 and 42 stop at Yerba Buena Road and San Felipe Road, 0.3 mile from the hike start/end. VTA bus 39 stops at San Felipe Road and Paseo de Arboles, 0.5 mile from the hike start/end. **Parking:** Free street parking is available around Evergreen Park.

This urban hiking route in San Jose's Evergreen neighborhood explores Evergreen Park, Montgomery Hill Park, and part of Evergreen Valley College. Two trails, the Yerba Buena Creek Trail and the Evergreen Creek Trail, unite these three areas.

The highlight of this route is Montgomery Hill, with its grasslands, views, and history. The hill is named for aeronautics pioneer John Joseph Montgomery. Starting in the 1880s, Montgomery began designing and flying gliders. In 1911, he built a monoplane glider called The Evergreen, and he made more than fifty glides right here in the Evergreen Valley. On October 31, 1911, however, The Evergreen stalled

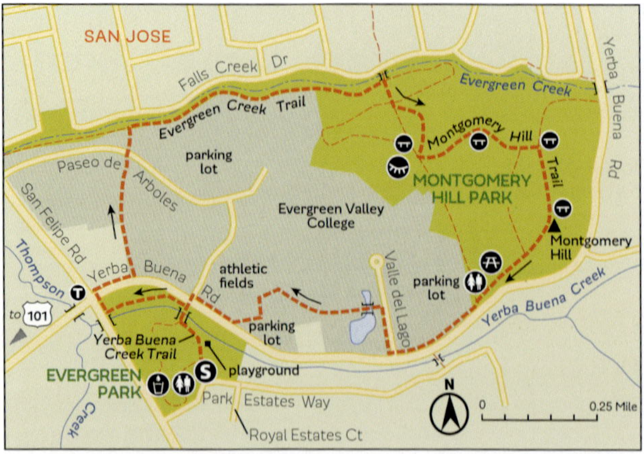

while flying less than 20 feet in the air. The glider crashed to the ground, and Montgomery hit his head on an exposed bolt and died two hours later. While his life was cut short, his accomplishments contributed to valuable advancements in the science of flight.

GET MOVING

Start the hike where Park Estates Way bends into a right angle west of Royal Estates Court. Enter Evergreen Park on a sidewalk near a restroom. This is the Yerba Buena Creek Trail. Pass the restroom and bear right to continue on the sidewalk past a playground. After 0.1 mile, head right and cross a bridge over Yerba Buena Creek. Once across the bridge, turn left on a wide dirt trail between the creek and Yerba Buena Road. The trail is shaded by oaks and toyons and lined with poison oak.

Continue straight for 0.2 mile. Then, turn right to reach the intersection of San Felipe Road and Yerba Buena Road. Cross Yerba Buena Road toward a shopping center and then turn right on a sidewalk just before the center. At 0.4 mile, turn left on a path through a grassy field. At 0.6 mile, cross Paseo de Arboles (no sign) and pick up a dirt trail just to your left. Then,

On Montgomery Hill, you'll learn how John Montgomery and San Jose played a role in the history of flight.

in 300 feet, turn right on a wide dirt trail. The first part of this trail is shaded by oaks, toyons, and buckeyes and lined with poison oak. The second part is exposed.

Continue 0.4 mile (until 1.1 miles total), ignoring turnoffs before this. Just before you reach a bridge on your left, turn right onto the Montgomery Hill Trail and head into Montgomery Hill Park. In 250 feet, continue straight at a junction. Just after this, ignore a trail branching off to the right; stay on the flatter, wider trail.

At 1.4 miles, arrive at an intersection where you can go right 250 feet to reach an overlook (not included in route mileage) or follow the selected route left. On this stretch, you'll see Evergreen College buildings in the foreground and downtown San Jose in the distance. You can also see Mount Umunhum and Loma Prieta to the southwest and Mount Tamalpais to the north. Over the next 0.4 mile, pass three areas with informational signage and benches (ignore turnoffs from the wide trail). At the third area, you've reached Montgomery Hill's summit at 594 feet. After the summit, descend 0.2 mile. Continue to the park exit on your left at some picnic benches.

Turn right and pick up a sidewalk along Yerba Buena Road (no sign) until you reach 2.1 miles. Turn right to enter the Evergreen Valley Community College campus at a nondescript entrance at Valle del Lago (no sign). After 175 feet, at a crosswalk, jog left, then right to walk toward a bridge.

At 2.2 miles, head left to cross the bridge over a pond. After the bridge, continue 0.2 mile on a wide paved path, passing by pickleball courts and continuing to a large parking lot. At the far end of the lot, turn left before the soccer stadium restrooms and walk 0.1 mile along and then through the lot. When you reach Yerba Buena Road (no sign), turn right.

Continue 0.1 mile and turn left at a crosswalk. Go straight briefly, then turn right on a wide dirt trail. After 50 feet, turn left to cross a bridge into Evergreen Park. After the bridge, turn left and return to the start.

40 Almaden Quicksilver County Park

DISTANCE: 6.1 miles
ELEVATION GAIN: 1,210 feet
HIGH POINT: 1,650 feet
DIFFICULTY: Challenging
TIME: 3 hours
FITNESS: Hikers, runners. Walkers can see Make It Shorter.
FAMILY-FRIENDLY: Families can see Make It Shorter, though this route still has 900 feet of elevation gain.
DOG-FRIENDLY: Yes, on leash
AMENITIES: Restrooms, benches, picnic benches, historical sites
CONTACT: Santa Clara County Parks

BEFORE YOU GO: Download the Almaden Quicksilver Historic Trail brochure created as an Eagle Scout project by Boy Scout Troop 466 at elcerritoscouting.org/wp-content/uploads/2021/03/Almaden-Quicksilver-Historic-Trail.pdf. It has detailed information on many of the sights you can see in this park. You may want to bring poles for the Deep Gulch Trail at the end of the route.

GPS: 37° 10' 26.1624" N, 121° 49' 30.018" W

GETTING THERE

Map to: Hacienda Entrance, Almaden Road, San Jose. **Parking:** Free parking is available at the Hacienda parking area and along Almaden Road.

Almadén, Spain, has the largest concentration of mercury (quicksilver) in the world and has been actively mined for over 2,000 years. When mercury was discovered in San Jose, this area became known as "New Almadén." Mining lasted between 1845 and 1976, and this was once the second-largest mercury mine in the world.

On this route, you'll spend 3 miles climbing more than 1,200 feet on wide fire trails and another 3 miles descending on a mix of fire trails and singletrack trails back to the start. On your way, you'll take in panoramic views and visit historic sites such as a mining tunnel, a mining camp, a giant furnace, and more. Note: Make sure you print out an Almaden Quicksilver Historic trail brochure before you visit (see Before You Go) for a deep dive on this park's history. I like to hike the route "backward" (according to the brochure) because the incline is more gradual and the route ends in the shade.

GET MOVING

From the Hacienda parking area, head uphill on the Mine Hill Trail, a wide fire trail. You'll be on this trail for a total of 2.8 miles.

Pass a four-way intersection at 0.4 mile, and at 1.2 miles, arrive at Capehorn Pass, another four-way intersection that's also a viewpoint over the Almaden Valley with a picnic bench and rest site. Here, go left and uphill on the Mine Hill Trail (now also the Bay Area Ridge Trail). At 1.6 miles, pass a junction with the Day Tunnel Trail on the right. Then, at 1.8 miles, stay right at a T; this is the end of the Bay Area Ridge Trail segment.

Continue on the Mine Hill Trail as you pass both ends of the April Trail over the next 0.2 mile. The April Trail (not included in route mileage) takes you to two historic sites: the April Tunnel Trestle, where ore was stored before processing, and the Powder House, where explosives were stored. At 2.5 miles, pass an intersection with the San Cristobal Mine Trail on your left that brings you to the San Cristobal Mine Tunnel, which you can walk into (not included in route mileage). Continue another quarter mile to Bull Run, where you'll find a T with an overlook and two picnic benches looking right at Mount Umunhum.

From here, take a quick detour to the Catherine Tunnel. Facing Bull Run, head right, and when the trail splits almost immediately in front of you, stay right. After a few hundred feet, complete a small loop. Here you'll reach a picnic bench and a jaw-dropping unobstructed view of the Almaden Valley. After this, head back to Bull Run at 3.1 miles.

Stay straight to pick up the Castillero Trail, a wide fire trail where you can enjoy some much-deserved time on a ridgeline. Enjoy sweeping westward views toward Mount Umunhum and Loma Prieta and intermittent eastward views toward Mount Hamilton. Ignore any unmarked turnoffs on your way, and at 3.8 miles, arrive at a large intersection. Continue just ahead to take in Almaden Valley views by a large tree, some agave plants, and a picnic bench.

Return back to the large intersection and turn left to take the Wood Road Trail toward the rotary furnace. This furnace

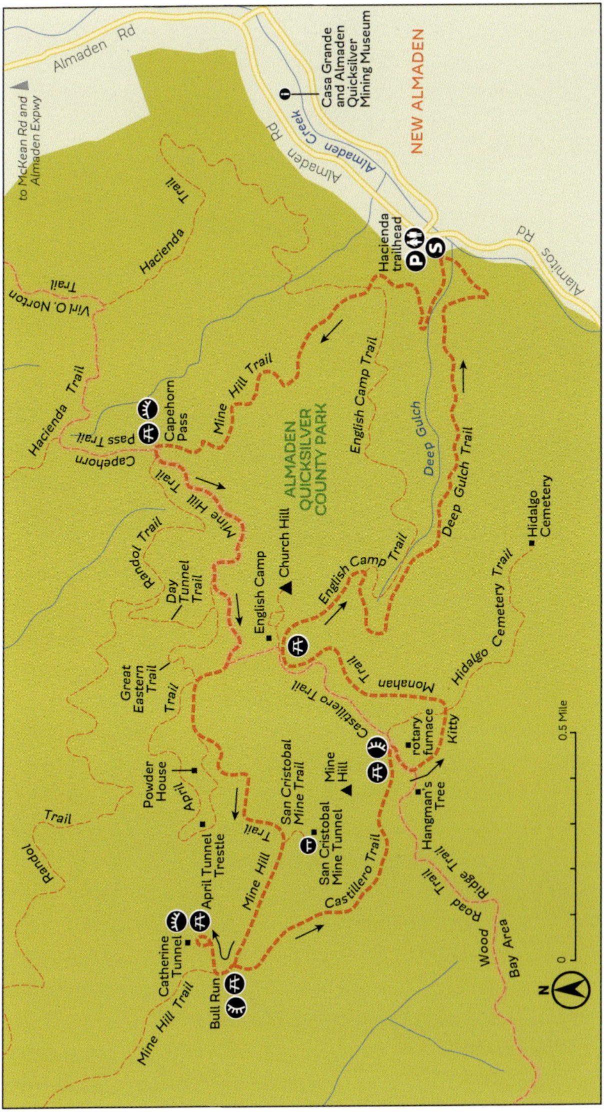
Almaden Rd
to McKean Rd and Almaden Expwy
Casa Grande and Almaden Quicksilver Mining Museum
NEW ALMADEN
Almaden Creek
Almaden Rd
Alamitos Rd
Hacienda trailhead
Hacienda Trail
Virl O. Norton Trail
Hacienda Trail
Mine Hill Trail
English Camp Trail
ALMADEN QUICKSILVER COUNTY PARK
Deep Gulch
Deep Gulch Trail
Capehorn Pass
Capehorn Pass Trail
Mine Hill Trail
Randol Trail
Day Tunnel Trail
Church Hill
English Camp
English Camp Trail
Hidalgo Cemetery
Hidalgo Cemetery Trail
Great Eastern Trail
Monahan Trail
Castillero Trail
rotary furnace
Kitty
Trail
Powder House
April
San Cristobal Mine Trail
Mine Hill
San Cristobal Mine Tunnel
Hangman's Tree
Ridge Trail
Trail
Randol
April Tunnel Trestle
Mine Hill Trail
Castillero Trail
Wood Road Trail
Bay Area
Catherine Tunnel
Bull Run
Mine Hill Trail
0
0.5 Mile
N

Bull Run is a perfect place to rest after a 2.8-mile incline on the Mine Hill Trail.

once helped reduce mercury from the ore fed into it. When you arrive at a junction after 450 feet, catch a glimpse of Hangman's Tree, the site of a nineteenth-century hanging, off to the right, then head left on the Kitty Monahan Trail. While there are different stories about who exactly was hanged here and why, people seem to agree that those in the know still throw stones at the tree to show their distaste for the crime the hanged man may have committed.

At 4.1 miles, head straight and downhill on the Kitty Monahan Trail at a junction with the Hidalgo Cemetery Trail. Here, the Kitty Monahan Trail is a singletrack trail surrounded by tall scrub plants. Continue downhill for a little under half a mile. As you pass a junction with the Castillero Trail, stay straight toward English Camp, an open area with a flagpole and some buildings. This is where English-speaking miners lived in the early mining days. Stay to the right of the flagpole, then head toward a tree with picnic benches at its base to pick up the English Camp Trail.

Follow this wide trail for a quarter mile, then turn right to pick up the shaded singletrack Deep Gulch Trail. There are some steeper downhill sections on this trail, so watch your footing. Continue along a creek here until you hit 5.9 miles total. As the trail emerges from the trees, head right toward a trail marker, then left at the marker. At the end of your descent, head left through a wide field back to the parking lot.

MAKE IT SHORTER

Walkers and families can do a 3.2-mile loop, taking the Mine Hill Trail and picking up the English Camp Trail on the left after 0.4 mile. They can visit English Camp and return on the Deep Gulch Trail. Note: This route still has more than 900 feet of elevation gain.

41 Joseph D. Grant County Park

DISTANCE: 7.5 miles
ELEVATION GAIN: 1,520 feet
HIGH POINT: 2,460 feet
DIFFICULTY: Challenging
TIME: 3 hours
FITNESS: Hikers, walkers, runners. Walkers can turn around after the viewpoint, take a flatter route in the park, or enjoy a picnic here.
FAMILY-FRIENDLY: See above.
DOG-FRIENDLY: Yes
AMENITIES: Restrooms, ranger station, campsites, picnic areas, benches, historic sites
CONTACT: Santa Clara County Parks
GPS: 37° 20' 7.6812" N, 121° 42' 58.7592" W

GETTING THERE

Map to: Joseph D. Grant County Park, 18405 Mt. Hamilton Road, Mt. Hamilton. **Parking:** There is a small entry fee for vehicles. Park in the Ranch House parking lot.

At nearly 11,000 acres, Joseph D. Grant County Park is the largest of Santa Clara County's regional park and recreation areas. The selected hike is designed to be long so that you can explore more of this vast park. To start, the route climbs to a viewpoint with a bench at 2,460 feet that looks over the Santa Clara Valley. Then it dips into Halls Valley, a valley between two ridges in the Diablo Range. Here you'll meander through oak-dotted grasslands with frequent views of Mount Hamilton and Lick Observatory. You'll also pass by the Snell Barn, named for Thomas E. Snell, who bought 700 acres here for dairy farming in 1856. Snell sold the ranch in 1911, and businessman and philanthropist Joseph D. Grant bought it in 1932 from the R. F. Morrow Land & Livestock company.

While you're here, get ready to see wildlife. I've seen butterflies, deer, jackrabbits, and wild pigs here, and thirty-two species of birds and thirty-nine species of mammals call this park home.

GET MOVING

From the Ranch House parking lot, head west along Grant Road. Enter the equestrian campground on your left after 0.1 mile. Exit the far end of the campground, cross the street, and pick up the Dutch Flat Trail at 0.2 mile (junction 56).

Head uphill on a wide fire trail lined with chaparral and oaks. (Watch out for poison oak.) As you climb, the chaparral shifts into grasslands. At 0.9 mile, stay right on the Dutch Flat Trail (also the Bay Area Ridge Trail) at junction 58. At 1 mile, head left at a T at an unmarked junction as the Heron Trail joins in from the right (junction 63). You are now on the Bay

Area Ridge Trail. Look for views of Mount Hamilton on your left. You'll stay on the Dutch Flat Trail for 3.9 more miles.

Continue uphill for 0.8 mile to a scenic overlook (2,460 feet elevation) with a picnic bench. From here, you take in views of San Jose, the Santa Clara Valley, and the Santa Cruz Mountains, including Mount Umunhum and Loma Prieta. On clear days, you can see as far as Mount Tamalpais, 60 miles north.

Over the next 2.7 miles, you'll climb rolling hills with intermittent views of the Santa Clara Valley, but overall you'll be trending downhill, descending over 750 feet in elevation in total. Enjoy tree cover for the last 0.3 mile of this stretch as you arrive at the southernmost part of the route (end of Bay Area Ridge Trail segment). You'll then continue on a relatively flat and shaded section of the Dutch Flat Trail for another half a mile.

Here you reach junction 62, where you head left to pick up the Brush Trail. Walk through some grasslands and reach junction 61 at 5.1 miles, where you turn right at a T. Head downhill, enjoying views of Mount Hamilton on your right. Oaks—some of them quite impressive in size—dot the landscape.

The Snell Barn is named for Thomas E. Snell, who bought land here in 1856.

At 5.6 miles, stay straight at junction 65 to pick up the Eagle Trail as it joins your trail from the right. This section of the route is pleasantly covered with oak trees, and there may be water here in the rainy season. At 5.9 miles, stay straight at junction 50 on the San Felipe Trail toward the Snell Trail. Exit the trees to see mountains to the right and the Snell Barn ahead and to the right. Toward the end of this stretch, stay on the trail as you pass two "Not a Trail" signs.

At 6.6 miles, reach junction 51, where you'll head right on the Snell Trail. Then, at 7.1 miles, continue on the Snell Trail at junction 82 as the Barn Trail joins from the right. At 7.4

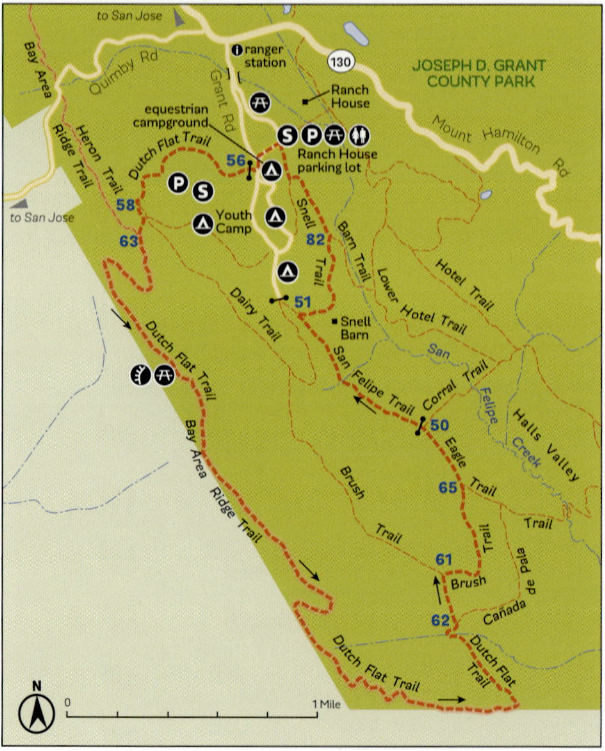

miles, stay on the Snell Trail as a trail with a fence branches off to the left. Then, 250 feet later, the Snell Trail merges with a paved trail that guides you back to the parking lot.

GO FARTHER

Visit the Joseph D. Grant ranch house and rose garden, located at the far end of the Ranch House parking lot. The house was constructed around 1881 and then remodeled and expanded by Joseph D. Grant in the 1930s.

42 Sierra Azul Preserve: Mount Umunhum

DISTANCE: 8.1 miles
ELEVATION GAIN: 1,200 feet
HIGH POINT: 3,489 feet
DIFFICULTY: Challenging
TIME: 3 hours
FITNESS: Hikers, walkers, runners. Walkers can hike around the summit, start their hike at the summit and descend as far as they like before turning around, or hike the Bald Mountain Trail (see Go Farther).
FAMILY-FRIENDLY: See above.
DOG-FRIENDLY: No
AMENITIES: Restrooms, shaded picnic area, Indigenous ceremonial space and other historic sites, overlook. No water is available on the trail, so bring enough to drink.
CONTACT: Midpeninsula Regional Open Space Preserve
BEFORE YOU GO: There are some accessible trails at the summit. *The Stories of Mount Umunhum* audio tour, a guide to the summit, is available as a YouTube Playlist. There is also a PDF guide you can download from the Midpeninsula Regional Open Space District website.
GPS: 37° 9' 34.776" N, 121° 52' 31.7928" W

GETTING THERE

Map to: Sierra Azul Open Space Preserve Bald Mountain parking lot, San Jose. **Parking:** Free parking. There are twenty-three standard spaces and one ADA space in the Bald Mountain parking lot. Four additional spaces line the road. The lot can fill up early. If necessary, you can park in the fifty-four-space lot at the top of the mountain and hike the route in reverse.

At 3,489 feet, Mount Umunhum is the fourth-tallest peak in the Santa Cruz Mountains. With a boxy radar tower at its summit, it's one of the easiest peaks to spot around San Jose. If you've hiked other routes in this book, you'll know I reference Mount Umunhum frequently—now it's time to climb it!

Umunhum means "hummingbird" or "resting place of the hummingbird" in five Ohlone languages. The hummingbird is the symbol of the Amah Mutsun Tribal Band and is part of their creation story, as legend says the bird brought them fire.

The out-and-back route winds steadily uphill with few intersections. You'll walk through chaparral, oaks, pines, and bay laurels, which provide shade but don't prevent you from enjoying views. You know you're close to the top when the trail exits the trees. Circle the summit to take in the views, read the informational signage, and visit the ceremonial circle before returning to the start.

GET MOVING

Start in the Bald Mountain parking area. Follow a paved sidewalk behind the restroom and cross the street to pick up the Mount Umunhum Trail. At 0.2 mile, you'll see Mount Umunhum's radar tower and a tower with a white sphere on top of it. At 0.3 mile, reach the Barlow Road junction. At this T, jog left, then right, to continue on the Mount Umunhum Trail. You are now on the Bay Area Ridge Trail. You'll soon get your first view of Mount Hamilton's Lick Observatory off to the right.

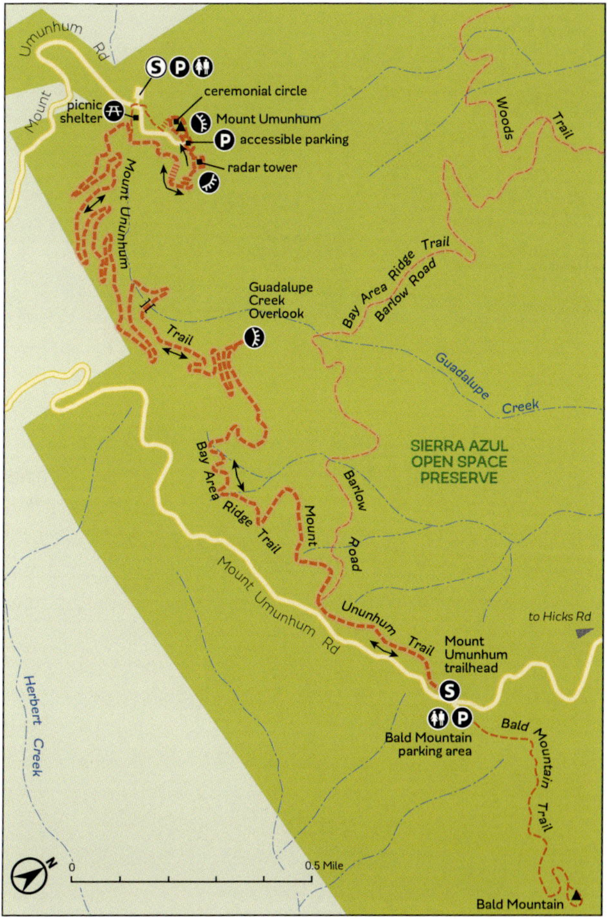

After a mile, reach the Guadalupe Creek Overlook, which you can visit with a quick roundtrip. The overlook has views north to San Jose and across to the Diablo Range. If you look up, you can peer toward the peak of Mount Umunhum. From this overlook, there are no intersections for a long stretch. You'll continue through the woods and cross Guadalupe Creek at 2 miles.

The views at the summit of Mount Umunhum stretch from the Pacific Ocean to the Sierra Nevada.

When a trail joins yours from the left at 3.6 miles, continue straight to hike the remaining stretch to the summit. You're very close when you arrive at a long set of stone steps. To learn about the summit, listen to *The Stories of Umunhum* audio guide on YouTube. You can also access a PDF with summit information on the Midpeninsula Regional Open Space District website.

At the summit, you'll come to a viewing area. Read informational signage here and take in views of San Jose, Mount Diablo and other Diablo Range mountains, Loma Prieta, and more. On clear days, you can even see San Francisco and even Oakland. Then continue to the eight-story building that was the base of a radar dish. From 1957 to 1980, this was the Almaden Air Force Station. The station closed in 1980 when satellite technology rendered the radar station obsolete.

Next, head to the ceremonial circle about 425 feet beyond the radar tower. This circle was placed here at the request of the Amah Mutsun Tribal Band as a space to hold ceremonies, pray, sing, and dance. The circle is ringed by stone blocks, which are marked with compass points to aid in ceremonial traditions. Mount Umunhum is sacred to the Indigenous people of California and particularly significant to the Amah Mutsun Tribal Band as this is the place of their people's creation story. After exploring this meaningful summit, return the way you came.

Note: If you need a restroom at the summit or want to eat in a covered picnic shelter, you'll start your return trip slightly differently. Pass the ceremonial circle and follow a flat, windy path and a stairway 500 feet down to the summit parking lot, where you'll find the restroom. Then cross Mount Umunhum Road at a crosswalk to pick up the Mount Umunhum Trail. After 100 feet, you'll reach the picnic shelter; soon after that, you'll be back on the main Mount Umunhum Trail. Follow the trail the way you came back to return to the start.

GO FARTHER

Got more miles in your legs? Check out the 1.4-mile roundtrip Bald Mountain Trail. This trail has just about 110 feet of elevation gain and offers sweeping views of the Santa Clara and Coyote Valleys.

43 Ed R. Levin County Park: Monument Peak

DISTANCE:	9.3 miles
ELEVATION GAIN:	2,410 feet
HIGH POINT:	2,594 feet
DIFFICULTY:	Difficult
TIME:	4.5 to 5 hours
FITNESS:	Hikers
FAMILY-FRIENDLY:	Families can take a short route on a paved trail from the parking area to Sandy Wool Lake.
DOG-FRIENDLY:	Yes, on leash
AMENITIES:	Restroom, picnic tables
CONTACT:	Santa Clara County Parks, East Bay Regional Park District
GPS:	37° 27' 26.586" N, 121° 51' 48.6972" W

GETTING THERE

Map to: City of Milpitas Dog Park at Ed R. Levin, Milpitas. **Parking:** There is a small entry fee for vehicles. Park near the City of Milpitas Dog Park at Ed R. Levin County Park.

Welcome to the longest hike in the book! As you climb up and down 2,594-foot Monument Peak, you'll get soaring views of San Jose, the Santa Clara Valley, the Santa Cruz Mountains, and even San Francisco and Oakland. You may see hang gliders and paragliders floating through the air and plentiful cows on the trails. Give the cows space when possible; they can charge if you get too close.

This hike can be busy at the start, but the crowds thin out as you climb. While there are moments of tree cover, this route is mostly in exposed grasslands, so plan your hike accordingly. It's especially beautiful on clear spring days when the grass is green. If you hike when it's hot, bring enough water for you and your four-legged friends.

Thanks go to County Supervisor Ed R. Levin, who fought to acquire this land as a park in the early 1960s so we can enjoy it today.

GET MOVING

Pick up the wide dirt Tularcitos Trail. Pass a junction at 0.1 mile, and at 0.2 mile, turn left and walk through a cattle gate to pick up the Agua Caliente Trail. At 0.7 mile, stay on the Agua Caliente Trail as you cross Launch Site Road. Pass through a cattle gate at 0.9 mile and then take either path when the trail splits at 1 mile (they quickly merge). Pass through two more cattle gates over the next quarter mile. Between these gates, you'll enjoy a bit of shade from oak trees at a seasonal creek crossing.

Stay to the right of a trail marker near a group of rocks at 1.4 miles, then continue to cross Monument Peak Road. Then, 425 feet later, reach a trail sign for the Monument Peak Trail to the Sierra Trail Junction. Just after this, walk through a

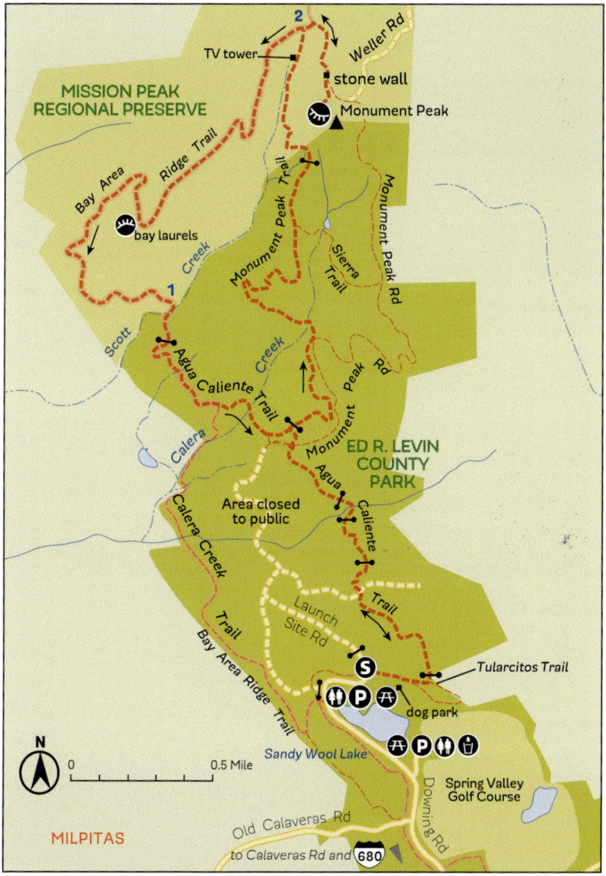

cattle gate and pick up the singletrack Monument Peak Trail for 0.6 mile (2.1 miles total). Here, enter an area with some large boulders, and make sure you continue far enough to see Monument Peak Road just to your right. You're on the right trail if your path stays narrow and looks at a rock formation beyond the trail. Do not go on the singletrack trail closer to the trees. Then, 0.1 mile after this, you'll reach a seasonal

Spring is the perfect season to climb Monument Peak. The weather isn't too hot and the hills are vibrant and green.

creek crossing. If your trail peters out after this crossing, you've crossed the creek at the wrong point. Turn around to find the right trail.

At 3 miles, stay on the Monument Peak Trail at a junction with the Sierra Trail. (There is no label on this trail marker.) Then, in a quarter mile, walk through a cattle gate. Stay left on the flat trail (not the unofficial trail that heads steeply uphill next to the gate). Just after this, you'll enter Mission Peak Regional Preserve.

At 3.7 miles, arrive at some KICU-TV satellite dishes and a tower. Then, about 0.1 mile later, turn right on a wide gravel road, Weller Road. You can see a large body of water, the Calaveras Reservoir, to the left and Rose Peak in the distance. Stay straight as Weller Road turns off to the left. Then, at 4.2 miles, reach the top of Monument Peak. On this final stretch to the summit, you'll see a mysterious stone wall of unknown origin, one of many found across the Bay Area. You can see another one in Sierra Vista Open Space Preserve (Hike 37).

Walk around the summit and enjoy the panoramic views atop Monument Peak. You can see the Santa Clara Valley, and you may spot paragliders in the air. When you're done at the summit, head back to where you picked up Weller Road (4.7 miles), catching a glimpse of Mount Diablo as you head back to this point. Stay straight to pick up the Agua Caliente Trail and head toward 9450 Weller Road. This is also part of the Bay Area Ridge Trail.

After 0.2 mile, descend steeply on the Bay Area Ridge Trail, ignoring the paragliding launch site to the right. At 5.7 miles, in the middle of the grasslands, take in some shade at a few bay laurel trees with rocks at their roots. Look north on a clear day, and you can see as far as San Francisco, Oakland, and Marin County.

At 6.8 miles, arrive at a Mission Peak marker 1, where you reenter Ed R. Levin County Park and cross a stream. Then, at 7 miles, go through a cattle gate. Continue straight on the Agua Caliente Trail at 7.4 miles. In 0.2 mile, the trail splits and you stay straight on the Agua Caliente Trail. Continue on this trail a little over 0.1 mile, ignoring a junction with the Monument Peak Trail on your left. At a four-way junction with Monument Peak Road, stay straight on the Agua Caliente Trail. In 275 feet, stay left at the trail marker near a group of rocks where you were before. Follow the Agua Caliente Trail to the Tularcitos Trail and return the way you came.

Next page: View of the Calero Reservoir (Hike 44)

MORGAN HILL, COYOTE VALLEY, AND GILROY

As you head south of San Jose, city quickly gives way to country. On the outskirts of San Jose in Calero County Park, you'll enjoy a walk through oak woodlands and grasslands, taking in views of the Calero Reservoir and a nineteenth-century Victorian home. Just down the road is Rancho Cañada del Oro, where you'll hike through more oak woodlands and grasslands with one adventurous creek crossing in winter.

Heading south, you reach the Coyote Valley, a narrow area between the Santa Cruz Mountains and the Diablo Range that is known for farmland, wildlands, and wildlife. Here you'll hike Coyote Valley Open Space Preserve's Arrowhead Loop among rolling hills, grasslands, and oak woodlands with views of the valley and surrounding mountains. Just across the valley, you'll visit Máyyan 'Ooyákma. You'll take in views from grassy hillsides and spot endangered butterflies and wildflowers on the Bay Checkerspot Trail. South of here, you'll find Coyote Lake–Harvey Bear Ranch County Park, where the Mummy Mountain Trail offers expansive Santa Clara Valley views from a serene singletrack trail.

The last two trails in this chapter are destination hikes that are worth the trip! Uvas Canyon County Park's Waterfall Loop is breathtaking after a winter rain, and Henry W. Coe is Northern California's largest state park. You'll take a moderate (and half-shaded) route to Frog Lake, a pleasant way to get acquainted with this park's 250 miles of trails.

44 Calero County Park

DISTANCE: 5.3 miles
ELEVATION GAIN: 730 feet
HIGH POINT: 1,000 feet
DIFFICULTY: Moderate
TIME: 2 hours and 15 minutes
FITNESS: Hikers, walkers, runners. The first 1.5 miles of the hike are relatively flat, so walkers can do this as an out-and-back route.
FAMILY-FRIENDLY: See above.
DOG-FRIENDLY: Yes, on leash on these trails, but not on all trails in the park
AMENITIES: Restrooms, picnic areas
CONTACT: Santa Clara County Parks
GPS: 37° 10' 30.954" N, 121° 45' 40.77" W

GETTING THERE

Map to: Calero County Park, 23205 McKean Road, San Jose.
Parking: Free parking in a large dirt lot.

Twenty miles south of downtown San Jose, just north of Rancho Cañada del Oro and Coyote Valley Open Space Preserve and just east of Almaden Quicksilver County Park, you'll find 4,417-acre Calero County Park. The park feels delightfully remote, and you'll spend your time here exploring grasslands and some oak woodlands while you take in views of nearby hills, the Santa Cruz Mountains and the Diablo Range, and Calero Reservoir.

For me, the highlights of this route come during the second half of this hike on the Los Cerritos and Oak Grove Trails. Here you'll enjoy views of the Calero Reservoir and see the Bailey–Fellows House, a historic Italianate Victorian home that is closed to the public. The home is named for Boanerges R. Bailey, who built this house around 1867, and Judge Edward Fellows, who lived in the home decades later in the 1940s.

The Los Cerritos Trail brings you through grasslands oak—dotted with views of the Calero Reservoir.

Most of the trails on this route are exposed. Avoid this park during hot summer days; instead, come in spring for green grass and wildflowers.

GET MOVING

Pick up the Oak Cove Trail across the street from the parking lot. At 0.2 mile, turn left at junction 4 to pick up the Figueroa Trail. This trail takes you through grasslands with some sections of oak woodlands. Enjoy the moments of shade: This is the only tree cover you'll get on the entire route. You'll be on the Figueroa Trail for just under 2 miles.

At 0.3 mile, stay right when you reach a T at junction 7. Stay straight after another 1.1 miles at junction 8. Then stay straight again at junction 9. Continue uphill a final 0.7 mile until you reach a four-way junction, junction 3, where you turn right on the Peña Trail.

From the Peña Trail, head uphill. As you climb, turn around to get views of Mount Umunhum. At 2.5 miles, you have reached the highest elevation on this route. Ignore a trail up to a water tower. Then, at 2.6 miles, turn left at junction 11 to pick up the Los Cerritos Trail. From here, take in your first eastward views toward the Coyote Valley.

Stay on the Los Cerritos Trail for 1.1 miles. After 0.4 mile here, you'll catch your first glimpse of the Bailey-Fellows House. As you continue, you'll see Mount Hamilton and the Calero Reservoir to your right and Mount Umunhum to your left. Reach junction 38 at 3.7 miles and continue straight to pick up the Oak Cove Trail. Stay straight again toward the Peña Trail at junction 39. You are now on a singletrack trail through grasslands with occasional oak trees and clear views of the reservoir.

Stay on the Oak Cove Trail for the remaining 1.6 miles of this route. You'll stay straight at junction 14 after 0.7 mile and straight again at junction 13 after another 0.3 mile. When you hit 5 miles, you'll encounter the Los Cerritos Pond rest site with a picnic spot. Then, at 5.1 miles, turn left at junction 4 to head back to the parking lot.

GO FARTHER

Visit the "Calero Bat Inn" on the Serpentine Loop, a "condo" that houses a breeding bat colony.

45 Rancho Cañada del Oro Open Space Preserve

DISTANCE: 4.2 miles
ELEVATION GAIN: 730 feet
HIGH POINT: 1,350 feet
DIFFICULTY: Moderate
TIME: 1 hour and 30 minutes
FITNESS: Hikers, walkers, runners. Walkers, see family-friendly option below.
FAMILY-FRIENDLY: Families with young children can hike the flat and accessible Llagas Creek Loop.
DOG-FRIENDLY: No
AMENITIES: Restrooms, picnic areas, accessible trail
CONTACT: Santa Clara Valley Open Space Authority
BEFORE YOU GO: Be prepared to cross a creek 4 miles into this route, which can be ankle-deep in the rainy season. It is easily passable in the dry season.
GPS: 37° 8' 41.1144" N, 121° 46' 44.6556" W

GETTING THERE

Map to: Rancho Cañada del Oro Open Space Preserve, 4289 Casa Loma Road, Morgan Hill. **Parking:** Free parking with around twenty standard spaces and two ADA parking spaces in the main parking lot. A larger overflow parking lot is 0.2 mile southwest along Casa Loma Road.

The route in Rancho Cañada del Oro is a pleasant mix of exposed and shaded trails.

Rancho Cañada del Oro, or "Golden Canyon Ranch," is a former walnut orchard purchased by the Peninsula Open Space Trust in 1999. The Longwall Canyon Trail, which comprises 1.4 miles of this loop hike, opened with the park in 2004. And the Mayfair Ranch Trail, which comprises the remaining 2.9 miles of the route, was added in 2007.

On this moderate loop, you'll walk through grasslands, chaparral, and oak woodlands. Starting on the Mayfair Ranch Trail, you'll climb 500 feet, enjoying views of the Santa Cruz Mountains and Diablo Range as you ascend. You'll then head downhill and continue your descent on the Longwall Canyon Trail. The Longwall Canyon Trail has similar habitats to the Mayfair Ranch Trail but includes a few creek crossings. It also enters neighboring Calero County Park. The route feels remote and peaceful. Wildflower displays are beautiful in spring, and there's enough shade to make the route hikeable even in summer.

GET MOVING

Pick up a paved path from the main parking lot behind the informational signage. After 100 feet, stay to the right of a

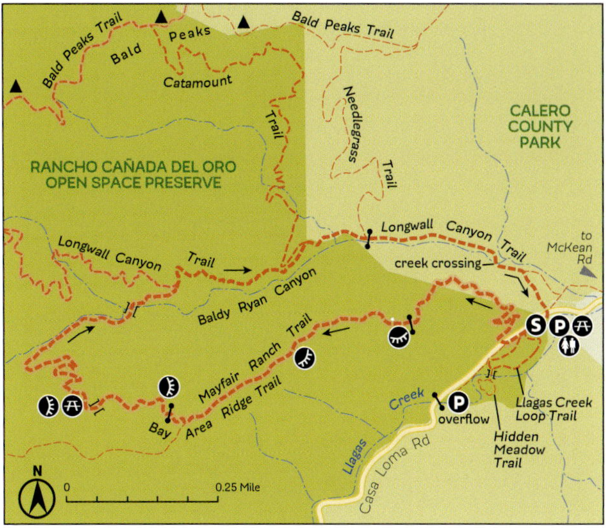

fence to pick up the dirt Mayfair Ranch Trail. (A left on a paved path would take you to the accessible Llagas Creek Trail.)

At 0.1 mile, cross Casa Loma Road and continue on the Mayfair Ranch Trail across the street. You are on this trail for 2.8 miles with no trail junctions. The first half of this stretch is uphill: you'll climb 500 feet in elevation walking through a mix of grasslands and woodlands filled with bay laurels, oaks, manzanitas, and poison oak.

When you reach 0.8 mile, walk through a gate and take in sweeping views of the Santa Cruz Mountains. At 1.2 miles, you enter an exposed area and get a nice view of Mount Umunhum. If you turn around, you can see the Diablo Range mountains. At 1.5 miles, just before heading back into the woods, look for a nice view of Mount Hamilton on your right.

At 1.6 miles, walk through a gate and catch a nice glimpse of Mount Umunhum on the left. At 1.9 miles, cross a bridge; soon after this, you'll reach a spot with a picnic bench that affords a view of Mount Hamilton. At 2.7 miles, cross a bridge over a creek called Baldy Ryan Canyon, which can be flowing or completely dry, depending on the time of year. At 2.8 miles, look right to see the ridge you just traversed. You've descended a lot since you were on it!

When you reach 2.9 miles, stay straight on the Longwall Canyon Trail, which features sections of exposed grasslands and oak woodlands. After half a mile, reach a T and turn right on the Longwall Canyon Trail. Then, at 3.6 miles, walk through a gate and stay straight to enter Calero County Park. As you walk along Baldy Ryan Canyon, you're in exposed grasslands.

At 4 miles, cross the creek again. While in summer this creek can be dry, in winter you may need to wade through ankle-deep water. Pass a trail marker about 200 feet after this and continue straight. A little under a quarter mile after the creek, reach a gate and head right to return to the parking lot.

GO FARTHER

For a challenge, try the Bald Peaks Loop. For something easier, try the accessible Llagas Creek Loop Trail.

46 Uvas Canyon County Park

DISTANCE: 5.1 miles
ELEVATION GAIN: 1,300 feet
HIGH POINT: 1,780 feet
DIFFICULTY: Moderate to challenging
TIME: 2 hours and 30 minutes
FITNESS: Hikers. Walkers can see Make It Shorter.
FAMILY-FRIENDLY: Families can see Make It Shorter.
DOG-FRIENDLY: No
AMENITIES: Restrooms, ranger station, picnic areas, benches, nature trail, waterfalls
CONTACT: Santa Clara County Parks

BEFORE YOU GO: Reserve a parking permit online before you hike (they book up early, and you may not have cell reception at the park). Get a Nature Trail brochure from the entry kiosk to guide you through the park's flora. One section of the Contour Trail closes after significant rainfall. Check the "Uvas Canyon County Park" page of the County of Santa Clara website for trail status.

GPS: 37° 5' 3.6744" N, 121° 47' 34.1844" W

GETTING THERE

Map to: Uvas Canyon County Park, 8515 Croy Road, Morgan Hill. **Parking:** Permit parking only. Get your parking permit at gooutsideandplay.org under "Day Passes."

Waterfall-filled Uvas Canyon is just the adventure you're looking for. You start out by visiting five waterfalls of varying sizes along the Swanson Creek and Waterfall Loop Trails. You then leave the waterfalls and creekside trails behind to see oaks, redwoods, Douglas-firs, bay laurels, and a sixth bonus waterfall on the Triple Falls Trail. You'll also get views of Knibbs Knob, the highest point in the park, and other surrounding hills.

If you're in the mood for something shorter, you can visit the first five waterfalls in just 2.2 miles. And for a little more distance and elevation, you can visit the same five waterfalls and turn your hike into a loop (see Go Farther and Make It Shorter for these options). The waterfalls run year-round but are much smaller in summer. The best time to visit is in winter after some rain when the waterfalls are flowing and ladybug clusters pop up along the trail. While remote, this park is popular, so expect crowds by the falls, especially in winter.

GET MOVING

From the parking lot, climb a flight of stairs and walk behind the restrooms. Follow a sign for the Waterfall Loop Trail. After 200 feet, reach a paved road where you bear right at another

Granuja Falls is one of six named waterfalls in Uvas Canyon County Park.

sign for the Waterfall Loop Nature Trail. Just before a paved bridge at 0.1 mile, head right and down a stairway to pick up the Swanson Creek Trail. Take the singletrack trail along the creek. Reach Lower Falls at 0.4 mile. Return the way you came to the paved bridge.

Cross the bridge, then turn left at 0.6 mile to start the Waterfall Loop Trail. Almost immediately, climb a stone stairway and cross a bridge over small but lovely Granuja Falls. At the top of the bridge, turn left on the wide Waterfall Loop fire trail.

At 0.7 mile and then shortly after, there are turnoffs to the left (one is unmarked, and the second is junction 7). Stay straight on the Waterfall Loop fire trail, heading uphill along the creek on a trail shaded by Douglas-firs and bay laurels.

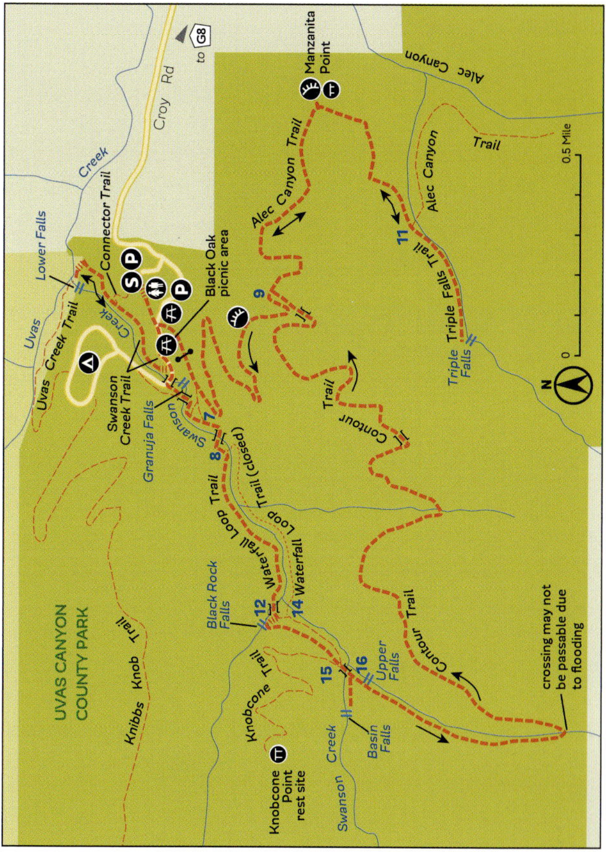

Cross another bridge and continue uphill at junction 8. (The creekside singletrack trail is closed here.)

Cross a bridge at 1 mile, then head right to visit Black Rock Falls at junction 12. As you face the waterfall, look for stone steps climbing alongside it. If you follow the stairs, you'll reach a trail that links you back with the fire trail at junction 14 at 1.1 miles. You can also stay on the fire trail instead of taking the stairway and trail alongside Black Rock Falls.

Continuing on the fire trail, reach the Knobcone Trail junction (junction 15) at 1.2 miles, where you stay straight. Cross a bridge, then head right toward Basin Falls at junction 16. After visiting the falls, return to junction 16 at 1.3 miles. This time, pick up the Contour Trail, a singletrack trail that heads steeply uphill. At the start of this stretch, pass Upper Falls, one of the wider falls in the park.

Continue to the creek crossing at 1.5 miles (which can be closed after heavy rains). At 2.5 miles, look left through the trees to see Knibbs Knob, the tallest point in this park (elevation 2,690 feet). Then, at 2.7 miles, look for Loma Prieta. About 250 feet after this, reach junction 9 for the Alec Canyon Trail. Head right here to exit the woods. You'll arrive at Manzanita Point, a scenic viewpoint with a bench, at 3.1 miles.

Reach the Triple Falls Trail (junction 11) after a quarter-mile, where you head straight and uphill. You're now on a wide trail surrounded by redwoods and running along a creek. Reach Triple Falls at 3.8 miles, then return to junction 9 at 4.5 miles. Continue straight at junction 9. Over the next 0.6 mile, enjoy a viewpoint over surrounding hillsides and the Diablo Range in the distance, then follow several switchbacks downhill. At the last Alec Canyon Trail marker, continue straight 200 feet toward a fence and the Black Oak picnic area. Then take a paved trail back to the parking area.

GO FARTHER

For a challenge, take the Knibbs Knob Trail to the top of Knibbs Knob. This is one of the steepest hikes in the Bay Area.

MAKE IT SHORTER

There are two easy ways to get a shorter waterfall hike in. For a 2.2-mile route, return to the start after visiting Upper Falls. And for a 3.4-mile route, you'll follow the directions above until junction 9, then skip to "Continue straight at junction 9."

47 Coyote Valley Open Space Preserve

DISTANCE:	4.1 miles
ELEVATION GAIN:	630 feet
HIGH POINT:	880 feet
DIFFICULTY:	Moderate
TIME:	1 hour and 30 minutes
FITNESS:	Hikers, walkers, runners
FAMILY-FRIENDLY:	May be best suited for older children due to the elevation gain.
DOG-FRIENDLY:	No
AMENITIES:	Restroom, benches, picnic area
CONTACT:	Santa Clara Valley Open Space Authority
GPS:	37° 10' 16.8924" N, 121° 43' 39.8208" W

GETTING THERE

Map to: 599 Palm Avenue, Morgan Hill. **Public Transit:** VTA Bus 68 stops at Santa Teresa Boulevard and Palm Avenue, a 0.7-mile walk to the preserve. **Parking:** Free parking in a large dirt lot.

Welcome to farm country, just 17 miles outside San Jose. Despite feeling like you're in a remote area, this trail is popular, and some locals use it as a daily workout. On this 4-mile loop with several hundred feet of elevation gain, you'll enjoy views of Máyyan 'Ooyákm, Henry W. Coe State Park, and the Diablo Range and cross five pedestrian bridges that can have water flowing under them in the rainy season.

This pleasant local route has found national importance: In 2015 it was certified by the National Park Service as an official site along the 1,200-mile Juan Bautista de Anza Trail, which stretches from Nogales on the US-Mexico border to San Francisco.

Oaks, buckeyes, and bay laurels dot the grassland landscape here. You may see deer, coyotes, or ground squirrels

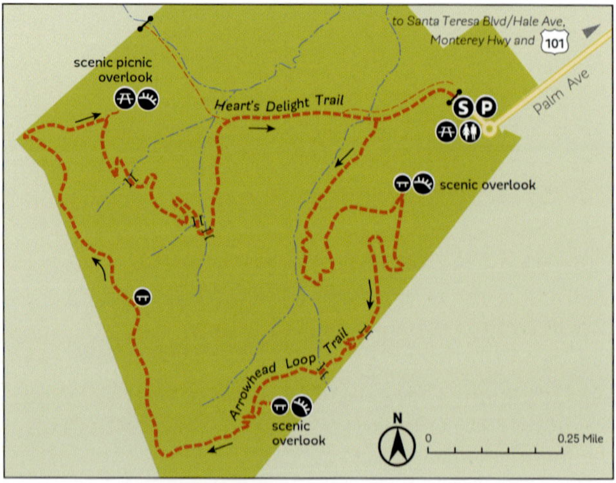

on the trail. You may also see cows that help graze the land for fire control. You probably can't get lost on this one-way trail, but I've noted directions, just in case. And if you notice a funky smell here, it's not due to the animal agriculture around you—it's a nearby mushroom farm.

GET MOVING

Pick up the gravel trail from the parking lot and walk past the informational signage. When you reach a cattle gate, walk through it to pick up the Arrowhead Loop Trail. At 0.2 mile, follow a sign to continue on the Arrowhead Loop Trail.

On this stretch, you're climbing through a wide grassland area dotted with oak trees and occasional patches of bay laurels. You can see Mount Hamilton's Lick Observatory off to the east. At 0.9 mile, head left at a trail junction to visit an overlook with a bench.

Continue along the loop, passing the first two of five bridges at 1.3 miles and 1.5 miles, then arrive at a turnoff for a scenic overlook with a bench at 1.7 miles. After visiting the overlook and its serene Coyote Valley views, continue straight on the Arrowhead Loop. Follow an arrow as the trail bends right at 2.0 miles. You're now 90% done with the climbing on this route. On this stretch, look for Loma Prieta and its towers to the left. You'll see the unincorporated town of Coyote down to your right and Henry W. Coe State Park (Hike 50) beyond the town.

At 2.9 miles, reach the turnoff for the scenic picnic overlook (this 500-foot roundtrip detour is not included in route mileage). If you need a break, the overlook has a few picnic benches with views of surrounding hillsides of the Coyote Valley. Take in the views here or keep going on the Arrowhead Loop Trail. Continue downhill on switchbacks, passing oaks and bay laurels and crossing the third bridge at 3.1 miles, and the fourth and fifth bridges in short succession. At 3.6 miles, reach the next trail marker and continue on the Arrowhead Loop Trail. At 3.9 miles, reach a trail marker pointing you back to the parking area.

The Arrowhead Loop's rolling hills make for a pleasant Coyote Valley route.

48 Coyote Lake–Harvey Bear Ranch County Park

DISTANCE:	3.9 miles
ELEVATION GAIN:	580 feet
HIGH POINT:	1,380 feet
DIFFICULTY:	Easy
TIME:	1 hour and 45 minutes
FITNESS:	Hikers, walkers, runners. Walkers and families can take the relatively flat Coyote Ridge Trail.
FAMILY-FRIENDLY:	Yes
DOG-FRIENDLY:	Yes, on leash
AMENITIES:	Portable toilet, benches, picnic benches
CONTACT:	Santa Clara County Parks
BEFORE YOU GO:	This hike is best in winter and spring when it's not too hot. Avoid hiking after a rain in winter. In spring, look for wildflowers.
GPS:	37° 4' 14.1204" N, 121° 31' 20.856" W

GETTING THERE

Map to: Mendoza Ranch parking, Coyote Lake–Harvey Bear Ranch County Park, Gilroy. **Parking:** Park at the Mendoza Ranch entrance. Plentiful free parking for cars (and just as many spaces for horse trailers).

Coyote Lake–Harvey Bear Ranch County Park is full of possibilities. This area is named for Coyote Lake, a large artificial lake for boating and fishing, and Harvey Bear, a previous landowner who deeded his cattle ranch to the Santa Clara County Parks and Recreation Department in 1997.

On this route, you'll hike a loop of the Mummy Mountain and Coyote Ridge Trails. The Mummy Mountain Trail gives you views of Coyote Lake, Gilroy, and the Santa Cruz Mountains. The macabre name comes from the shape of the ridge: Some say it looks like a reclining mummy with its head to the north and body to the south. While the Mummy Mountain

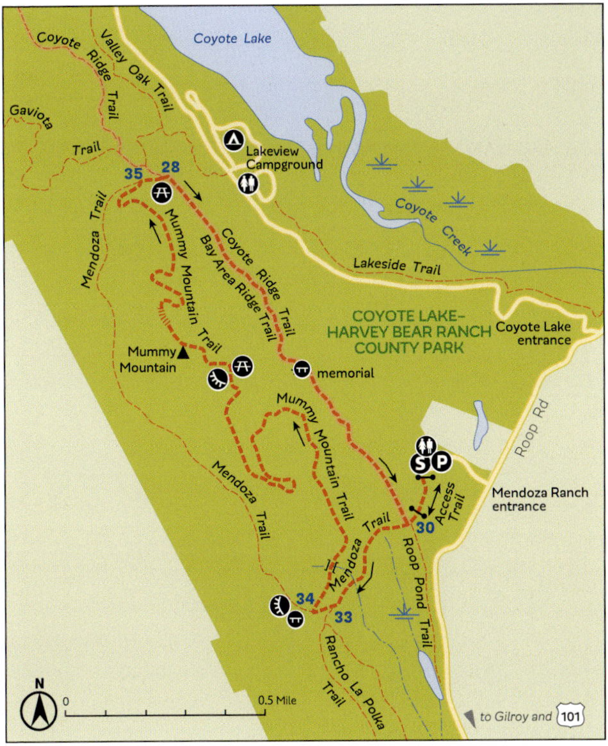

Trail has some elevation gain, the return trip on the Coyote Ridge Trail (also part of the Bay Area Ridge Trail) is pleasantly flat. It's not uncommon to spot deer and cattle here, but while there's a notice about wild pigs at the trail entrance, I haven't seen any on my hikes.

GET MOVING

Walk through a cattle gate to pick up the Access Trail. After 0.1 mile, pass through another cattle gate, ignoring the Roop Pond Trail on your left. When you arrive at junction 30 just after this, stay straight to pick up the Mendoza Trail. Head

Mummy Mountain Trail offers expansive views across the Coyote Valley.

uphill through oak woodlands that open up into grasslands. At 0.4 mile, reach junction 33, where you stay straight and head uphill on the Mendoza Trail.

When you soon come upon junction 34, turn right on the Mummy Mountain Trail. There are benches here to take in the panoramic westward views over Morgan Hill, Gilroy, and the southern Santa Clara Valley. The Mummy Mountain Trail is a singletrack trail with sections of oak woodlands and open grasslands. You'll be on this trail for just over 2 miles without any trail junctions, ascending 350 feet in elevation in 1.4 miles and descending those same 350 feet in the remaining 0.7 mile.

This stretch includes several highlights to watch out for, starting with a lovely wood bridge on a shady section of the trail at 0.6 mile total. At 0.9 mile, keep an eye out for a tall sandstone formation with holes in it on your left, and at 1.4 miles, you'll catch your first glimpse of Coyote Lake before reaching sweeping views of the city of Gilroy, Mount Umunhum, and Loma Prieta. You can stop for a rest and a snack at a picnic table looking over Coyote Lake at 1.9 miles before gearing up for your descent, which starts shortly after this point. At 2.1 miles, you'll descend a stone stairway to be greeted by valley views. And at 2.5 miles, you'll be rewarded with more sparkling lake views.

The Mummy Mountain Trail drops you off at junction 35, where you turn right on the Mendoza Trail. Continue downhill for 400 feet, then turn right on the Coyote Ridge Trail at junction 28. You are now on the Bay Area Ridge Trail. You'll be on this gravel fire road for a mile (until 3.7 miles total). Most of this trail is in open grasslands, and while your path runs along the lake, you don't see much of it. You'll encounter some minor ups and downs here, but it's flat compared to the first half of the hike. Halfway through this stretch, you'll come across an area with benches and a memorial to a family killed in a plane crash on the hillside above you. When you arrive at junction 30, turn left and use the Access Trail to return to the parking lot.

GO FARTHER

Return on the Mendoza Trail instead of the Coyote Ridge Trail to add more elevation to your route, or visit another time and hike more of the Bay Area Ridge Trail here. On any visit, you can finish your hike with a picnic near Coyote Lake.

49 Máyyan 'Ooyákma–Coyote Ridge Open Space Preserve

DISTANCE: 5.2 miles
ELEVATION GAIN: 1,010 feet
HIGH POINT: 1,320 feet
DIFFICULTY: Moderate
TIME: 2 hours and 30 minutes
FITNESS: Hikers, walkers, runners. Walkers can do an out-and-back walk on the Bay Checkerspot Trail, which is less steep than the Serpentine Spring Trail, or they can take the easy and accessible Máyyan Wáayi Overlook Trail.
FAMILY-FRIENDLY: See above.
DOG-FRIENDLY: No

AMENITIES: Restrooms, overlooks, and picnic tables. The Máyyan Wáayi Overlook Trail is accessible.

CONTACT: Santa Clara Valley Open Space Authority

BEFORE YOU GO: Get a Butterfly Pass online on the Santa Clara Valley Open Space Authority website. You can also do this on your phone once you're at the park. Days and hours of operation change seasonally. Please check the preserve's page of the Santa Clara Valley Open Space Authority website for current schedules. Free docent-led tours are required on weekends during wildflower season (March to May). Please clean your shoes at the cleaning station before going on the trails.

GPS: 37° 12' 52.0776" N, 121° 43' 16.9536" W

GETTING THERE

Map to: Máyyan 'Ooyákma, 9611 Malech Road, Morgan Hill.
Parking: Free parking in a lot with forty-two parking spaces, including ADA spaces.

Máyyan 'Ooyákma, meaning "Coyote Ridge" in the Chochenyo language of the Muwekma Ohlone Tribe, opened to the public in August 2023. Situated in the narrowest section of land between the Santa Cruz Mountains and the Diablo Range, this is an important habitat for tule elk, the threatened Bay checkerspot butterfly, and other wildlife. Wildflowers thrive here, especially on the Bay Checkerspot Trail. To minimize impact on weekends during wildflower season, the Santa Clara Valley Open Space Authority runs docent-led tours in the park.

On this loop route, you'll climb 800 feet on the Serpentine Spring Trail over 1.3 miles. You'll then walk along a ridge and the Tule Elk Trail for another 1.3 miles. Lastly, you'll descend 800 feet in 2.2 miles on the Bay Checkerspot Trail. Highlights of this trail include almost 4 miles on the Bay Area Ridge Trail, the potential for wildlife sightings, and views of the Coyote Valley, surrounding mountains, and neighboring parks. Lowlights include views of US 101 and sounds from a nearby shooting range.

Spring wildflowers are abundant on the Bay Checkerspot Trail.

GET MOVING

Before you get started, here are three things to note about this route. First, there are mile markers about every 0.2 mile so that you can keep track of your progress. Second, on each of the three trails on this route, there are shade structures where you can escape the heat on warm days and learn about the park's flora, fauna, geology, and history. Finally, the route is straightforward. Once you get onto the Serpentine Spring Trail, there are no turns aside from the ones you're supposed to make to stay on the route, so if you like, get on the trail and enjoy—no directions needed! However, if you prefer more guidance, read on.

The views on this route start in the parking lot, where you can spot Loma Prieta and Mount Umunhum in the distance. From the lot and facing a hill, head left and pick up the Serpentine Spring Trail. After 200 feet at an overlook, stay right to continue on the Serpentine Spring Trail.

Climb uphill on a wide dirt trail through grasslands. As you ascend, you can see Coyote Peak in Santa Teresa County

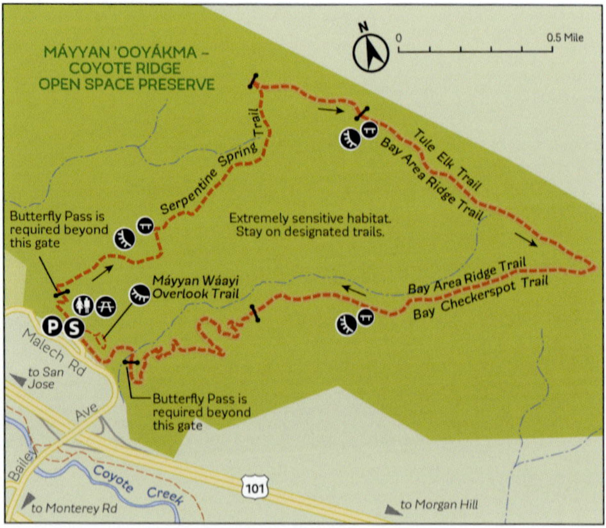

Park (Hike 35), Communications Hill (Hike 38), downtown San Jose, Coyote Valley farmland, Coyote Valley Open Space Preserve's Arrowhead Loop (Hike 47), US 101, and El Toro. On this stretch, you gain 800 feet of elevation—80% of the elevation of the full route.

At 1.3 miles, turn right on the Tule Elk Trail, a wide, flat trail through grasslands. You'll get closer views of the Diablo Range on the left. At 2.6 miles, pick up the Bay Checkerspot Trail. Here you face the Coyote Valley and can see Calero County Park (Hike 44) below Loma Prieta. This trail starts out wide, then narrows and heads steeply downhill. At 4.8 miles, turn right on a wide gravel trail. Continue for almost half a mile back to the parking lot, crossing a tributary of Coyote Creek on your way.

MAKE IT SHORTER

Check out the Máyyan Wáayi Overlook Trail, a short, accessible trail with views and picnic benches.

50 Henry W. Coe State Park

DISTANCE: 5.3 miles
ELEVATION GAIN: 810 feet
HIGH POINT: 3,010 feet
DIFFICULTY: Moderate
TIME: 2 hours and 30 minutes
FITNESS: Hikers, walkers, runners. Walkers and families can take the Flat Frog Trail to and from Frog Lake.
FAMILY-FRIENDLY: See above.
DOG-FRIENDLY: No
AMENITIES: Restrooms, visitor center, benches, picnic benches, campgrounds
CONTACT: California State Parks
BEFORE YOU GO: When you arrive at the park, check in at the visitor center and pay the parking fee by cash or credit card. Consider bringing hiking poles for some sections of this route.
GPS: 37° 11' 14.028" N, 121° 32' 49.7184" W

GETTING THERE

Map to: Henry W. Coe State Park Visitor Center, Coe Ranch Campground, 9000 E Dunne Avenue, Morgan Hill. **Parking:** There is a parking fee per car. There are small parking lots before and after the visitor center. Parking can fill up fast on spring and holiday weekends.

Welcome to Henry W. Coe's former ranch and the largest state park in Northern California! With 250 miles of trails, you'll need multiple trips to this park to truly start to know it. This moderate loop to and from Frog Lake is a nice way to get acquainted.

On this route, you'll take a combination of singletrack and fire roads to reach the lake, visiting a memorial bench and the Henry Coe monument along the way. On the return trip, you'll take relatively flat singletrack trails that offer moderate

shade. The shade makes it possible to hike reasonably comfortably, even on hot days. Some unique aspects of this hike are the entire route's elevation, which is above 2,400 feet, and the interesting flora here, which includes ponderosa pines and giant manzanitas. The fire roads are well maintained, but the singletrack trails can be overgrown, so be on the lookout for poison oak, thistles, and ticks.

GET MOVING

Start the hike on Manzanita Point Road, just uphill from the visitor center and across from a small parking area. Take the paved road, walking by the park residence and toward a gate. To the left of the gate, pick up the Monument Trail, a singletrack trail winding through grasslands with occasional tree cover by pines, oaks, and manzanita trees. On the sections with tree cover, watch out for poison oak. You'll climb over 300 feet in elevation on this first stretch. This is the most challenging part of the hike.

At just under half a mile, at a Monument Trail marker, turn left on the Ponderosa Trail and walk just under 0.2 mile to Eric's Bench. This is a memorial for Morgan Hill resident Eric David May, who fell to his death at age twenty-six after summiting Mount Shasta in 1988. For more of a walk, you can complete a small 0.6-mile loop on the Ponderosa Trail after the bench (not included in selected route mileage).

Return to the Monument Trail marker where you turned onto this trail. You're now at 0.8 mile. Head straight on the Ponderosa Trail. At just under 1 mile, cross Hobbs Road and arrive at the Henry Coe monument. When Coe's daughter Sada Coe Robinson gifted this ranch to Santa Clara County in 1953, she stipulated that a monument be dedicated to her father, that the ranch become a park for Californians, and that money raised from the land go to the park's development as a recreational area.

After visiting the monument, return to Hobbs Road and turn right, heading uphill on the wide fire road. At 1.1 miles, pass the other end of the Monument Trail. Continue on this road, where you'll descend 425 feet in elevation. This is a good place to break out your hiking poles, as there are loose rocks here. Early on in this stretch, look for views of Mount Hamilton's Lick Observatory. More oaks, pines, and giant manzanitas line the trail.

At 1.9 miles, continue straight on Hobbs Road toward Frog Lake as you cross Little Coyote Creek, which can be dry depending on the season. (You will come back to this point later.) Then, at 2.1 miles, turn right off Hobbs Road toward Frog Lake. Here you'll find a restroom and picnic bench. Descend and head past a trail marker to walk along

Frog Lake marks the halfway point of this route through Henry W. Coe State Park.

the southern end of the lake. The lake isn't too big, but it's nice to see water on a hot day. When you're done, head back to the trail marker (2.2 miles total) and take a left just after it to head toward Coe Headquarters.

This singletrack trail is shaded and lined with poison oak, so watch what you touch. At 2.4 miles, reach the junction with Little Coyote Creek where you were before. This time, turn left on the Flat Frog Trail just after the creek. Stay on this trail until you reach 4.7 miles total. You'll snake around a creek with a nice amount of shade provided by oaks, bay laurels, manzanitas, and pines. You'll also encounter a few stairs about halfway through this stretch.

At 3.9 miles, you'll want to look left for Mount Sizer, the park's highest peak at 3,216 feet. About 0.1 mile later, you'll come to a bench that's a nice place to rest. At 4.7 miles, cross Manzanita Point Road and continue straight toward Coe Headquarters via the Corral Trail. After 250 feet, turn right on the Corral Trail at a T shortly after this. Follow this trail 0.6 mile back to the visitor center.

GO FARTHER

Hike the 0.6-mile Ponderosa Trail Loop after Eric's Bench, or for a longer return trip, or take the Middle Ridge, Fish, and Corral Trails for a 6.6-mile hike. And for a true challenge, hike Mount Sizer!

ACKNOWLEDGMENTS

A BOOK IS NEVER A SOLO ENDEAVOR, and it takes a village to bring a book to fruition. I did my first hike for this book in 2022 and my last one in 2024, and the editing work went well into 2025. During this years-long stretch, many people came together as part of my village to make this book a reality.

First, I'd like to thank my 18th Street family for their patience on those many, many days when I clipped the leash on the dog and disappeared for hours after saying, "I'll be out hiking for a bit. See you soon!" Many of the hikes were an hour and change from my house in San Francisco, so even a 3-mile route would mean I was gone for three to four hours at a time.

My mother Maxine explored many routes with me, narrowly escaping a rattlesnake in Ed R. Levin Park. She put lots of babysitting hours in, along with other favorite babysitters Came and Graciela. Brett, my partner, came on most of the routes with me. We saw giant redwoods, dodged charging cows, and did two birthday hikes together. Dylan, our sweet and curious kiddo, was very understanding when mommy needed to go out hiking. Somewhere during the writing of this book, she began to love hiking herself, and now regularly asks for 9-mile hikes and 30,000 steps on her Fitbit.

I also want to thank many friends and family members for joining me on a hike, including Alexandra Friedman, Nadia Gil, Ksenya Gusak, Mary Herne, David Kenin, Jean and Bruce Lider, and Tanya Loh. Special mention goes to my crew who went out on more than one route with me: Darryl and Jenny Grove, Samuel Klatchko, Clayton LaPointe, Debbie Mansfield, Tikva Morowati, Natasha Hopps, Nanette Rowe, Debby Wang, and John Wiley.

So many people come out of the woodwork—friends, friends of friends, people I had never met before—to test out routes for my book. Huge thanks go to Théophile Aries, Katie Cook, Rachel Garb, Natalya Etina, Ramona Esquivel, Johnny Fu, Thibault Jousse, Guy Joaquin, Ramya Kaushik, Dan Luscher (who took great photos and tested out transit-friendly routes), Carrie Marquez, Meghan Pearse, and Linda Vergas. And this book literally would not be possible without Yasaman Mohsenin, who tested twenty-eight of my routes. Your notes, feedback, and photos have improved this book for the better.

Of course, none of this would be possible without the support of the wonderful folks at Mountaineers Books who entrusted me with a third book project. Thank you to Susan Elderkin, who shepherded me through the book-writing process, and Sarah Currin, my copyeditor, for finding all the edits I wouldn't have found myself. And it was a pleasure to work with Ben Pease after admiring his mapmaking work for many years!

Lastly, I want to thank all the land managers in this book for tirelessly answering my questions about every nuance on maps, trail signs, trail names, and more. Thank you for making sure my descriptions were as accurate as possible.

TRAILS BY TYPE

EASY

- 2 Mori Point
- 5 Pillar Point Bluff and Mavericks Beach
- 6 Sawyer Camp Trail
- 24 Baylands Nature Preserve
- 25 Sunnyvale Bay Trail
- 27 Picchetti Ranch Open Space Preserve
- 28 Stevens Creek County Park
- 38 Communications Hill
- 39 Evergreen Urban Hike
- 48 Coyote Lake–Harvey Bear Ranch County Park

MODERATE

- 1 Milagra Ridge
- 2 Mori Point
- 3 Sweeney Ridge
- 7 Fifield-Cahill Ridge Trail
- 8 Edgewood County Park and Nature Preserve
- 9 Pulgas Ridge Open Space Preserve
- 10 Huddart Park
- 11 Wunderlich County Park
- 13 El Corte de Madera Creek Preserve
- 14 Upper La Honda Creek Open Space Preserve
- 16 Russian Ridge Open Space Preserve
- 17 Skyline Ridge Open Space Preserve
- 19 Los Trancos Open Space Preserve
- 20 Long Ridge Open Space Preserve
- 21 Enid W. Pearson-Arastradero Preserve
- 22 Stanford Dish
- 23 Foothills Nature Preserve

26 Rancho San Antonio
27 Picchetti Ranch Open Space Preserve
29 Fremont Older Open Space Preserve
30 Montalvo Arts Center
31 Sanborn County Park
32 St. Joseph's Hill Open Space Preserve
35 Santa Teresa County Park
36 Alum Rock Park
37 Sierra Vista Open Space Preserve
44 Calero County Park
45 Rancho Cañada del Oro Open Space Preserve
47 Coyote Valley Open Space Preserve
49 Máyyan 'Ooyákma–Coyote Ridge Open Space Preserve
50 Henry W. Coe State Park

CHALLENGING AND DIFFICULT

2 Mori Point
4 Pedro Point Headlands and Devil's Slide
7 Fifield-Cahill Ridge Trail
12 Purisima Creek Redwoods Preserve
15 Windy Hill Open Space Preserve
18 Monte Bello Open Space Preserve
33 Bear Creek Redwoods Open Space Preserve
34 Castle Rock State Park
40 Almaden Quicksilver County Park
41 Joseph D. Grant County Park
42 Sierra Azul Preserve: Mount Umunhum
43 Ed R. Levin County Park: Monument Peak
46 Uvas Canyon County Park

1 TO 3 MILES

1 Milagra Ridge
2 Mori Point
28 Stevens Creek County Park

30 Montalvo Arts Center
38 Communications Hill
39 Evergreen Urban Hike

3 TO 6 MILES

3 Sweeney Ridge
4 Pedro Point Headlands and Devil's Slide
5 Pillar Point Bluff and Mavericks Beach
6 Sawyer Camp Trail
8 Edgewood County Park and Nature Preserve
9 Pulgas Ridge Open Space Preserve
10 Huddart Park
11 Wunderlich County Park
13 El Corte de Madera Creek Preserve
14 Upper La Honda Creek Open Space Preserve
16 Russian Ridge Open Space Preserve
17 Skyline Ridge Open Space Preserve
18 Monte Bello Open Space Preserve
19 Los Trancos Open Space Preserve
20 Long Ridge Open Space Preserve
21 Enid W. Pearson-Arastradero Preserve
22 Stanford Dish
23 Foothills Nature Preserve
24 Baylands Nature Preserve
25 Sunnyvale Bay Trail
26 Rancho San Antonio
27 Picchetti Ranch Open Space Preserve
29 Fremont Older Open Space Preserve
31 Sanborn County Park
32 St. Joseph's Hill Open Space Preserve
33 Bear Creek Redwoods Open Space Preserve
34 Castle Rock State Park
35 Santa Teresa County Park
37 Sierra Vista Open Space Preserve

44 Calero County Park
45 Rancho Cañada del Oro Open Space Preserve
46 Uvas Canyon County Park
47 Coyote Valley Open Space Preserve
48 Coyote Lake–Harvey Bear Ranch County Park
49 Máyyan 'Ooyákma–Coyote Ridge Open Space Preserve
50 Henry W. Coe State Park

MORE THAN 6 MILES

6 Sawyer Camp Trail
7 Fifield-Cahill Ridge Trail
12 Purisima Creek Redwoods Preserve
15 Windy Hill Open Space Preserve
36 Alum Rock Park
40 Almaden Quicksilver County Park
41 Joseph D. Grant County Park
42 Sierra Azul Preserve
43 Ed R. Levin County Park

WITH LOTS OF ELEVATION GAIN (700+ FEET)

3 Sweeney Ridge
4 Pedro Point Headlands and Devil's Slide
7 Fifield-Cahill Ridge Trail
9 Pulgas Ridge Open Space Preserve
10 Huddart Park
11 Wunderlich County Park
12 Purisima Creek Redwoods Preserve
13 El Corte de Madera Creek Preserve
14 Upper La Honda Creek Open Space Preserve
15 Windy Hill Open Space Preserve
16 Russian Ridge Open Space Preserve
17 Skyline Ridge Open Space Preserve
18 Monte Bello Open Space Preserve
23 Foothills Nature Preserve

26 Rancho San Antonio
27 Picchetti Ranch Open Space Preserve
29 Fremont Older Open Space Preserve
31 Sanborn County Park
32 St. Joseph's Hill Open Space Preserve
33 Bear Creek Redwoods Open Space Preserve
34 Castle Rock State Park
35 Santa Teresa County Park
36 Alum Rock Park
37 Sierra Vista Open Space Preserve
40 Almaden Quicksilver County Park
41 Joseph D. Grant County Park
42 Sierra Azul Preserve: Mount Umunhum
43 Ed R. Levin County Park: Monument Peak
44 Calero County Park
45 Rancho Cañada del Oro Open Space Preserve
46 Uvas Canyon County Park
49 Máyyan 'Ooyákma–Coyote Ridge Open Space Preserve
50 Henry W. Coe State Park

REDWOOD HIKES

10 Huddart Park
11 Wunderlich County Park
12 Purisima Creek Redwoods Preserve
13 El Corte de Madera Creek Preserve
14 Upper La Honda Creek Open Space Preserve
30 Montalvo Arts Center
31 Sanborn County Park
33 Bear Creek Redwoods Open Space Preserve

HIKES NEAR WATER (RESERVOIRS, LAKES, THE BAY, THE OCEAN, OR WATERFALLS)

2 Mori Point
4 Pedro Point Headlands and Devil's Slide

URBAN HIKES

HIKES WITH THE BEST VIEWS

HIKES TO AVOID IN SUMMER

18 Monte Bello Open Space Preserve
29 Fremont Older Open Space Preserve
35 Santa Teresa County Park
37 Sierra Vista Open Space Preserve
41 Joseph D. Grant County Park
43 Ed R. Levin County Park: Monument Peak
44 Calero County Park
48 Coyote Lake–Harvey Bear Ranch County Park

HIKES WITH THE BEST WILDFLOWERS

2 Mori Point
8 Edgewood Park and Natural Preserve
9 Pulgas Ridge Open Space Preserve
14 Upper La Honda Creek Open Space Preserve
15 Windy Hill Open Space Preserve
16 Russian Ridge Open Space Preserve
21 Enid W. Pearson-Arastradero Preserve
26 Rancho San Antonio
37 Sierra Vista Open Space Preserve
44 Calero County Park
45 Rancho Cañada del Oro Open Space Preserve
47 Coyote Valley Open Space Preserve
48 Coyote Lake–Harvey Bear Ranch County Park
49 Máyyan 'Ooyákma–Coyote Ridge Open Space Preserve

ADDITIONAL SAN JOSE TRAILS

THERE ARE MANY MORE TRAILS to hike in the City of San Jose. Below is a list of just some of these trails. This is not meant to be exhaustive, as San Jose is adding to these trails all the time. The trails here don't require turn-by-turn directions, so just choose a trail and start exploring!

Trail Name	Distance	Terrain	Notes
Albertson Parkway	0.5 mile	Paved and accessible	Connects the Santa Teresa neighborhood to Santa Teresa County Park.
San Francisco Bay Trail	0.8 mile	Paved and accessible	CA-237 Bikeway between Los Esteros Road and Coyote Creek is part of the Bay Trail and the Juan Bautista De Anza National Historic Trail.
Calero Creek Trail	1.9 miles	Paved between Los Alamitos Creek and Harry Road (0.7 mile) gravel between Harry Road and the Stiles Ranch Trail (1.2 miles) at Santa Teresa County Park	Runs between Singer Park and Santa Teresa County Park. The Stiles Ranch Trail is inaccessible during the rainy season.
Coyote Creek Trail	19.7 miles in three seg-ments	Mostly paved	One day, this will be one of San Jose's longest trail systems, reaching from the Bay to San Jose's southern boundary.
Evergreen Creek	1.2 miles	Dirt	Runs along Montgomery Hill Park. Take some of this trail on the Evergreen Urban Hike (Hike 39).

Trail Name	Distance	Terrain	Notes
Guadalupe Creek Trail	1.7 miles	Gravel	Runs along the creek and some ponds. An easy point to pick up the trail is Almaden Lake Park.
Guadalupe River Trail	11.4 total miles	Mix of paved and gravel	Mileage split across two spans (9 miles along northern/central reach and 2.4 miles along southern reach). A highlight is a stretch in Guadalupe River Park.
Lake Almaden Trail	0.6 mile	Paved and accessible	Follows the banks of Lake Almaden. Connects to the Guadalupe River Trail to the north and the Los Alamitos Creek Trail to the south.
Lake Cunningham Trail	2 miles	Paved and accessible	Loop Trail that circles Lake Cunningham.
Los Alamitos Creek Trail	4.7 miles	Paved and accessible	Includes two street crossings at Graystone Lane and Camden Avenue.
Los Gatos Creek Trail	11.2 miles	Paved	1.9 miles from San Carlos Street to Lonus Street. Also 9.3 miles from Meridian Avenue to Lexington Dam in Los Gatos. Includes some on-street connections.
Odette Morrow Trail	1 mile	Paved and accessible	Paved loop trail Shady Oaks Park and along Coyote Creek.
Penitencia Creek Trail	2.8 miles	Mix of paved and gravel	Go on some of this trail in the Alum Rock Park (Hike 36).
Saratoga Creek Trail	0.8 mile	Paved and gravel	Runs parallel to Lawrence Expressway but with creek views.
Silver Creek Valley Trail	4 miles	Paved	Follows Silver Creek and roads within the Silver Creek Country Club neighborhood. Some segments of the trail are quite steep.

Trail Name	Distance	Terrain	Notes
Thompson Creek Trail	2.9 miles	Paved and gravel	Follows Thompson Creek.
Umbarger Parkway	0.6 mile	Paved and accessible	Follows Umbarger Road and Barberry Lane on either side of US 101.
Upper Silver Creek Trail	0.9 mile	Paved and accessible	Links Silver Creek Linear Park with the upper picnic area.
Yerba Buena Creek Trail	0.9 mile	Unpaved	Runs along the creek in Evergreen Park along Estates Way to Silver Estates Drive.

RESOURCES

Bay Area Ridge Trail
https://ridgetrail.org
(415) 561-2595

California State Parks
www.parks.ca.gov

City of Half Moon Bay
www.half-moon-bay.ca.us
(650) 726-8255 (Recreation Services)

City of Palo Alto
www.cityofpaloalto.org
(650) 329-2100

City of San Jose
www.sanjoseca.gov
(408) 535-3500

County of San Mateo
www.smcgov.org
(650) 363-4161

Evergreen Valley College
www.evc.edu
(408) 780-0420

Golden Gate National Recreation Area
www.nps.gov/goga
(415) 561-4700

Midpeninsula Regional Open Space District
www.openspace.org
(650) 691-1200

Pacifica Land Trust
www.pacifica-land-trust.org
(650) 260-4772

San Francisco Bay Trail (Metropolitan Transportation Commission)
https://mtc.ca.gov/operations/regional-trails-parks/san-francisco-bay-trail
(415) 778-6700

San Francisco Public Utilities Commission (SFPUC)
www.sfpuc.gov
(415) 554-3289

Santa Clara County Parks
https://parks.santaclaracounty.gov
(408) 355-2200

Santa Clara Valley Open Space Authority
www.openspaceauthority.org
(408) 224-7476

Stanford University
https://dish.stanford.edu
thedishinfo@lists.stanford.edu

SRI International
www.sri.com
(650) 859-2000

INDEX

Opposite: Observing a tafoni formation in Castle Rock State Park (Hike 34)

ABOUT THE AUTHOR

Alexandra Kenin grew up in Wyckoff, New Jersey, and is proud to be a Jersey girl. She studied French and business at Georgetown University, then spent a few years working and playing in New York City. While living in New York, she took a fateful vacation to San Francisco, which influenced her to move to the City by the Bay.

But before making it out west, she had some more work to do. She earned an MBA from the Wharton School and an MA from the Lauder Institute, both at the University of Pennsylvania. After graduating, she moved to San Francisco and worked as a product marketing manager at Google for nearly five years.

After leaving Google, she began exploring the city, eventually coming up with the idea for her urban hiking tour company, Urban Hiker SF. Urban Hiker SF explores the stairways, hills, trails, and history of the city. Since 2012, the company has led tours for thousands of hikers from dozens of countries.

Alexandra is passionate about travel and tries to visit a new country every year (she's up to fifty-one so far). When she's not traveling or out on the trails, she lives in San Francisco with her partner, Brett, their child, Dylan, and their dog, Jodie.

OTHER TITLES YOU MIGHT ENJOY FROM MOUNTAINEERS BOOKS

Urban Trails: San Francisco
Coastal Bluffs · The Presidio · Hilltop Parks & Stairways
Alexandra Kenin

Urban Trails: East Bay
Oakland · Berkeley · Fremont · Richmond
Alexandra Kenin

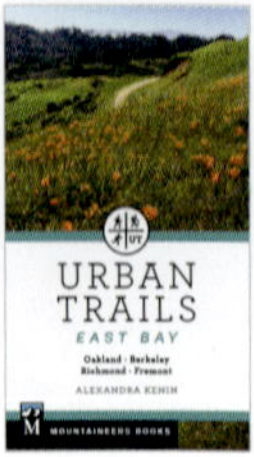

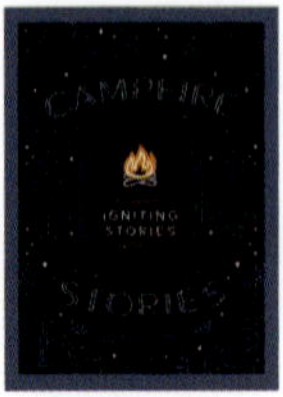

Campfire Stories Deck
Prompts for Igniting Stories by the Fire
Ilyssa Kyu and Dave Kyu

Dirty Gourmet
Food for Your Outdoor Adventures
Mai-Yan Kwan, Emily Nielson, and Aimee Trudeau

www.mountaineersbooks.org